This is a superb study of an important Old Testament book. The author is thoroughly acquainted with the text and makes relevant notes to enable the reader to apply what happened in Nehemiah's day to his or her life today. This study will enrich the lives of those who read it.

—David Denyer, PhD, emeritus professor of Old Testament,
Nyack College and Alliance Theological Seminary

Les Tripp has given us a timely resource for believers who seek to advance the kingdom of God. His lessons from the book of Nehemiah are an encouragement to all of us to stay the course under trying circumstances. *Walls and Gates* provides down-to-earth insights into carrying out God's plan in our personal life and ministry. This book will help everyone who reads it build strong walls and effective gates.

—Joel Wiggins, DMin, PhD, president, Crown College

Walls and Gates is an impressive, in-depth examination of the determination and leadership of Nehemiah! This volume is a practical blueprint for establishing a healthy, productive spiritual life and effective disciple-making ministry. Disciples are called to build healthy churches. This devotional study translates Nehemiah's actions into twenty-first century terms and urges believers to persist in their faith and in advancing Christ's kingdom.

—Chuck Brewster, founder and president, Champions
of Honor, author of *Dead Men Rising*

Les Tripp shines a spotlight on Nehemiah's determination and sound direction in carrying out a very difficult task. In so doing, he encourages believers to step up to their responsibilities as disciples. *Walls and Gates* applies the trials Nehemiah faced to one's personal calling, faith, and spiritual service.

—Marty Granger, founder and president, Ministry Alliance

The Lord has called his people to be passionate in building the body of Christ into vibrant, healthy, reproducing communities. In *Walls and Gates*, Les Tripp has captured with clear understanding, how Nehemiah's actions can be applied today in responding to that call. We must take faith-filled risks, both personally and as communities of believers, to advance his kingdom. It is only by an ever-growing dependence on the Lord that we can navigate through the conflicts, opposition, and diversions mounted by today's culture. A must read for every disciple.

—Fred G. King, lead pastor, Ensley Alliance Church

Walls and Gates is a practical weapon in the arsenal of every believer and every ministry. Each section details the principles for succeeding in developing a personal hedge of protection and advancing ministries in the face of obstacles. Les Tripp understands that when believers exercise strong faith, they are victorious in their personal life, relationships, and ministry.

—Craig Stephen Smith, president, Tribal Rescue Ministries, Inc., and author of *It's a Beautiful Thing, Indigenous Faith, Miracle at Mile Marker 313*, and *Whiteman's Gospel*

Walls *and* Gates

A Devotional Study of the Book of Nehemiah

LES TRIPP

ISBN: 978-1-967375-44-8 (Paperback)
ISBN: 978-1-967375-45-5 (E-book)

Library of Congress Control Number: 2024901175

Printed in the United States of America

Published by:

THE QUIPPY™ QUILL

info@thequippyquill.com
(302) 295-2278

This book is dedicated to the wife of my youth, my soul mate, and my chief encourager. Her patience and unselfish support were significant in seeing this effort through. I could not have done it without her.

CONTENTS

TABLES AND FIGURES

PREFACE

I enjoy Old Testament stories about how God did extraordinary things through ordinary people. One of those people is Nehemiah and his leadership in restoring the walls and gates of Jerusalem and restoring the people to their covenant relationship with the Lord. I did a study of the book of Nehemiah 15 years ago and wanted to revisit the book. My purpose this time, was to take a deeper look at Nehemiah's response to God's call, his actions in the face of opposition and how these lessons can be applied today. What began as a focus on personal spiritual walls and gates broadened to include principles for establishing effective spiritual walls and gates in the community of believers.

In this book, we will explore Nehemiah's call by God, his leadership in restoring the walls and gates, and his actions in leading the people back to their covenant relationship with the Lord.

Today, while we may not construct physical walls and gates around our cities, we desperately need personal, spiritual walls and gates. We need to construct a robust bulwark to defend ourselves from outside attacks and sturdy gates to control what we let into our lives. Nehemiah provides a clear process that we can apply personally and in our faith community.

As we follow Nehemiah, we will stop along the way to challenge readers to consider both personal and Christian community applications.

Scriptures are taken from the English Standard Version, unless otherwise noted.

I am indebted to Dr. David Denyer for his suggestions for making this work more informative, and to Trish Rollins, Steve Bracken, my wife, Linda, and my daughter, Diane, for their detailed attention and excellent suggestions in improving readability.

INTRODUCTION

And they said to me, "The remnant there in the province who had survived the exile is in great trouble and shame. The wall of Jerusalem is broken down, and its gates are destroyed by fire." (1:3)

Nebuchadnezzar besieged Jerusalem in 597 BC and moved the upper elements of the Jewish society to Babylon. In 587 BC, he returned to Jerusalem, destroyed the walls, and burned the temple.[1] There appear to have been several failed attempts to rebuild the walls in the 142 years between their destruction and the arrival of Nehemiah.[2]

The Importance of Walls and Gates

Physical Walls and Gates. Walls have always been about protection from outsiders or privacy. Physical gates are used to control access to cities or property. In Bible times, gates were also places where business was conducted (Ruth 4:1–6).

Spiritual Walls and Gates. We are products of what we allow into our lives, either good or bad. We are flooded by images and sounds and their associated emotional responses. We are influenced by our relationships and environment. We are confronted with distractions (the world), temptations (the flesh), and misdirection (the devil). We are engaged in spiritual warfare as we seek to obey the Lord and follow his guidance. As believers we need effective walls to keep us from being overwhelmed by our culture and the trials and tribulations of life. We need strong, guarded gates to control what we let in.

Our first line of defense is the wall of salvation. Isaiah prophesied that "In that day this song will be sung in the land of Judah: We have a strong city; he sets up salvation as walls and bulwarks" (Isaiah 26:1). Once assured of our salvation, we need to allow the Holy Spirit to guard what comes into our lives and to empower us to be effective in advancing his kingdom.

> We have a strong city; he sets up salvation as walls
> and bulwarks. Open the gates, that the righteous
> nation that keeps faith may enter in. You keep him
> in perfect peace whose mind is stayed on you,
> because he trusts in you. (Isaiah 26:1–3)

The book of Nehemiah also provides a pattern for advancing a personal ministry and service in a community of believers. It begins with hearing and responding to God's call, defining that call, bathing it in prayer, developing or joining a team, and moving forward. Moreover, the book deals with being persistent in the face of resistance, objections, and obstacles. In our communities of believers, there is a need, as in Nehemiah's day, for making spiritual transformation a priority.

> So then you are no longer strangers and aliens,
> but you are fellow citizens with the saints and
> members of the household of God, built on the
> foundation of the apostles and prophets, Christ

Jesus himself being the cornerstone, in whom the whole structure, being joined together, grows into a holy temple in the Lord. In him you also are being built together into a dwelling place for God by the Spirit. (Ephesians 2:19–22)Unless the LORD builds the house, those who build it labor in vain. Unless the LORD Watches over the city, the watchman stays awake in vain. (Psalm 127:1)

Historical Context

From the time of Moses (Deuteronomy 28) through the prophets, the Lord warned the children of Israel what would happen if they failed to keep the Law. Because they failed in their obedience to the Lord, his judgment became increasingly severe. Eventually he brought judgment on Israel, the Northern Kingdom. The Assyrians captured the Northern Kingdom in 701 BC, removed and integrated the people into their culture.[3] One hundred years later, Nebuchadnezzar captured Judah and Jerusalem and took the Jews into captivity. After seventy years, Cyrus released the Jews to return to Jerusalem and Judea. The following is a generally accepted chronology of these events and Nehemiah's role.

Table 1: Chronology of Events Related to Nehemiah's Time

Year (BC)	Event
740–722	The Assyrians captured Israel (the Northern Kingdom).
701	The Assyrians failed to capture Jerusalem and Judah.

597	Nebuchadnezzar captured Jerusalem.
586	Nebuchadnezzar destroyed the temple and the walls.
539	Cyrus captured Babylon.
537	Cyrus released Jews. (The first group of exiles returned.)
465	Artaxerxes ascended the throne of Persia.[4]
458	Ezra returned to Jerusalem. (The second group of exiles returned.)
445	Nehemiah was released to go to Jerusalem in the month of Nisan
445	The walls were completed and dedicated in the months of Elul and Tishri.
433	Nehemiah returned to Susa.[5]
424	Nehemiah returned to Jerusalem.[6]

The Principle Events in the Narrative

Nehemiah's journal begins with his hearing about the conditions in Jerusalem and King Artaxerxes releasing him to go to Jerusalem. He departed Susa (Persia) in the month of Nisan, 445 BC. It took from six to eight weeks for him to make the 765-mile journey to Jerusalem. We are not informed when he began rebuilding the walls, but we know the walls were completed in fifty-two days (at the end of Elul; 6:15).

The Festival of Booths and a solemn assembly (chapters 8–10) took place in the month of Tishri, immediately following the completion of the walls. The dedication of the walls followed at the end of Tishri or at the beginning of Cheshvan.

Nehemiah's first term as governor of Judah was twelve years, from 445 to 433 BC. (See 5:14 and 13:6.) The dates of his second term are uncertain. John MacArthur believes his second term began in 424 BC. One commentator indicates that the words "And after some time I asked leave of the king ..." (13:6) could mean after a period of years.[7] Nehemiah may have been absent about nine years. His second term ended before 407 BC, when records indicate that Bagohi was governor of Judah.[8]

Table 2: Hebrew and Gregorian Calendars[9]

Hebrew		Gregorian
1	Nisan	March–April
2	Lyar	April–May
3	Sivan	May–June
4	Tammuz	June–July
5	Av	July–August
6	Elul	August–September
7	Tishri	September–October
8	Chesvan	October–November
9	Kislev	November–December
10	Tevel	December–January
11	Shevat	January–February
12	Adar	February–March

THE CHALLENGE

Facing Impossibilities

The words of Nehemiah the son of Hacaliah. Now it happened in the month of Chislev, in the twentieth year, as I was in Susa the citadel, that Hanani, one of my brothers, came with certain men from Judah. And I asked them concerning the Jews who escaped, who had survived the exile, and concerning Jerusalem. And they said to me, "The remnant there in the province who had survived the exile is in great trouble and shame. The wall of Jerusalem is broken down, and its gates are destroyed by fire. As soon as I heard these words I sat down and wept and mourned for days, and I continued fasting and praying before the God of heaven. (Nehemiah 1:1–4)

1

Nehemiah faced an impossible situation. There was nothing he could do. He was more than seven hundred miles from Jerusalem. He did not have authority to go or to act.

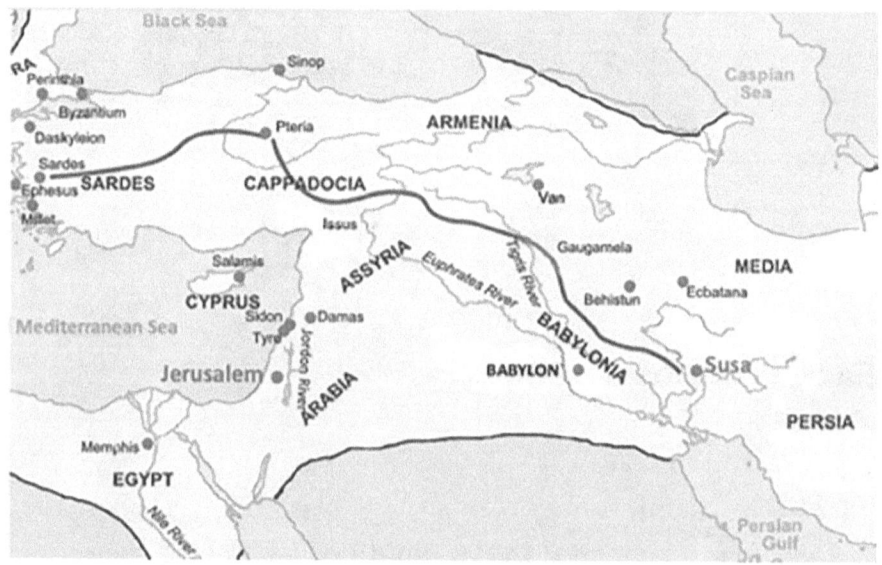

Figure 1: The Persian Empire in the Time of Nehemiah

Nehemiah's response was to humble himself before God and express deep concern over the situation in Jerusalem. He responded by weeping, fasting, and praying. Weeping is most often associated with grief. It is a profound emotional reaction to a great loss. Of course, real men do not weep, right? He was not able to do anything about the situation and he was grieved over the condition of his homeland. One facet of fasting is the denial of anything that interferes with our connection to the Lord. It is an act that intensifies the connection with the Lord.

For Nehemiah, prayer was the intentional act of pleading his case before the Lord and listening for a response. Nehemiah put the problem in the Lord's hands. He had a close relationship with the Lord.

We often face challenges that seem impossible—be it in relationships, work, or service to the Lord. Our tendency is to view the world through human eyes and human abilities. As believers, we are called to look at the world through eyes of faith. There are many passages in scripture that proclaim the Lord's sovereign power over things that seem impossible. Jesus reminded his disciples that dealing with the impossible requires faith.

> With men this is impossible, but with God all things are possible. (Matthew 19:26)

Personal Walls: Do you know the God of impossibilities? Do you have a personal relationship with him? Do you grieve over broken places? Are you afraid to be profoundly broken before the Lord? Is fasting and prayer your normal response to challenges? Are you burdened with a need that puts you on your knees?

Community Walls: When others face impossible situations, do you point them to the God of possibilities, to a personal relationship with God? Do you come alongside those who are grieving? Do you grieve with them? Are you a source of encouragement?

When challenged, a disciple turns first to the Lord.

Praying over the Impossible

> And I said, "O LORD God of heaven, the great and awesome God who keeps covenant and steadfast love with those who love him and keep his commandments, let your ear be attentive and your eyes open, to hear the prayer of your servant that I now pray before you day and night for the people of Israel your servants, confessing the sins of the people of Israel, which we have sinned against you. Even I and my father's house have sinned. We have acted very corruptly against you and have not kept the commandments, the statutes, and the rules that you commanded your servant Moses. Remember the word that you commanded your servant Moses, saying, 'If you are unfaithful, I will scatter you among the peoples, but if you return to me and keep my commandments and do them, though your outcasts are in the uttermost parts of heaven, from there I will gather them and bring them to the place that I have chosen, to make my name dwell there.' They are your servants and your people, whom you have redeemed by your great power and by your strong hand." (Nehemiah 1:5–10)

Nehemiah prayed about conditions in Jerusalem. Yet that is not where he began his prayer.

He began by acknowledging the sovereignty and faithfulness of the God to whom he is praying.

He continued by confessing his sins and the sins of the people.

He described the consequences of the people's unfaithfulness.

He claimed God's promises of restoration. He interceded for the people.
And he asked God to hear his prayer and the prayers of the people.

For Nehemiah, prayer was more than laying out a list of wants and needs. He understood the sovereignty of God and focused on it as it applied to the Israelites. Only then did he address his immediate concern: broken walls and gates. Jesus instructed his listeners this way:

> Do not be like them, for your Father knows what you need before you ask him. Pray then like this: "Our Father in heaven, hallowed be your name …" (Matthew 6:8–9)

Personal Walls and Gates: When you face a challenge, is this the way you pray? Do you begin by recognizing to whom you are praying, his conditions for a relationship, and his promises? Do you address God or just the situation? Do you jump to the bottom line? Do you stop to acknowledge that he is God and you are not?

Community Walls and Gates: Do you model this prayer when bearing the burdens of others? Do you direct their attention to the Lord and his promises?

A disciple knows to whom he prays.

Praying Over the Plan

> O Lord, let your ear be attentive to the prayer of your servant, and to the prayer of your servants who delight to fear your name, and give success to your servant today, and grant him mercy in the sight of this man. Now I was cupbearer to the king. (Nehemiah 1:11)

The seventh and last part of Nehemiah's prayer was to ask God to grant him success in petitioning King Artaxerxes.

When the Babylonians captured Jerusalem and Judea, they took the leadership and top elements of society back to Babylon. Some captives became a part of the king's court. For example, both Daniel and Nehemiah held important positions in the king's court. Nehemiah was the king's cupbearer. He was responsible for ensuring that the wine served to the king was not poisoned. As such, he was a highly trusted confidant of the king.

Nehemiah's access to the king gave him an opportunity to plead the case of the broken walls and gates in Jerusalem.

Recall that Nehemiah had been fasting and praying over the situation for days. Perhaps during these days of prayer, the Lord revealed a plan to him. Jeremiah tells us that God has a plan.

For I know the plans I have for you, declares the LORD, plans for welfare and not for evil, to give you a future and a hope. (Jeremiah 29:11)

Personal Walls and Gates: Do you hear from God in your quiet time? Is your prayer life a two-way conversation? Does the Lord speak to you through his Word?
Community Walls and Gates: Are you listening as you pray for others? Do you share with others what the Lord is saying to you?

**A disciple keeps an open channel of
communication with the Lord.**

Be Alert

In the month of Nisan, in the twentieth year of King Artaxerxes, when wine was before him, I took up the wine and gave it to the king. Now I had not been sad in his presence. And the king said to me, "Why is your face sad, seeing you are not sick? This is nothing but sadness of the heart." Then I was very much afraid. (Nehemiah 2:1–2)

Four months passed between Nehemiah hearing about the conditions in Jerusalem (the month of Chesvan) and the opportunity to meet with Artaxerxes (the month of Nisan). Nehemiah's grief had become a burden and it was obvious when he came into the presence of the king.

Artaxerxes was quick to notice Nehemiah's emotional state. He recognized that Nehemiah was heartbroken. It was not a physical problem. Jesus promises comfort in times of sorrow.

> Blessed are those who mourn, for they shall be comforted. (Matthew 5:4)

Personal Walls and Gates: Do you try to keep your emotions under cover? Do you tell people things are going well when they are not?

Community Walls and Gates: Do you notice when people are experiencing difficulties? Do you observe a change in their countenance? Do you let them know what you are seeing?

A disciple is alert to the needs of others.

Fear Not

> And the king said to me, "Why is your face sad, seeing you are not sick? This is nothing but sadness of the heart." Then I was very much afraid. I said to the king, "Let the king live forever! Why should not my face be sad, when the city, the place of my fathers' graves, lies in ruins, and its gates have been destroyed by fire?" Then the king said to me, "What are you requesting?" So I prayed to the God of heaven. And I said to the king, "If it pleases the king, and if your servant has found favor in your sight, that you send me to Judah, to the city of my fathers' graves, that I may rebuild it." (Nehemiah 2:2–5)

Students of Persian culture say that a person was not to show sadness in front of the king. Therefore, Nehemiah was deeply afraid knowing that he could not hide his emotions. Yet his obvious grief gave opportunity to explain why he was sad and what was needed.

Nehemiah prayed again before replying to the king. When he responded, he mentioned the tombs of his fathers. He may have been appealing to the importance the Persians placed on the tombs of their ancestors.

The apostle John tells us that we can come boldly to God.

> And this is the confidence that we have toward him, that if we ask anything according to his will he hears us. And if we know that he hears us in whatever we ask, we know that we have the requests that we have asked of him. (1 John 5:14–15)

Personal Walls and Gates: Do you lay a solid prayer foundation before starting tasks? When you face the impossible, do you sense that God wants to work through you?

Community Walls and Gates: When others sense God's calling on their lives, do you join them in prayer for clarity of thought and wisdom in pursuing that calling? Are you able to affirm the calling?

Disciples are set apart by their confidence in the Lord.

Petition for Release

And I said to the king, "If it pleases the king, and if your servant has found favor in your sight, that you send me to Judah, to the city of my fathers' graves, that I may rebuild it." (2:5)

Nehemiah petitioned the king for release from his duties as cupbearer and permission to go to Jerusalem to rebuild the walls and gates.

Mark tells us that Jesus left the crowds to which he had been ministering so he could minister in new areas.

And they found him and said to him, "Everyone is looking for you." And he said to them, "Let us go on to the next towns, that I may preach there also, for that is why I came out." And he went throughout all Galilee, preaching in their synagogues and casting out demons. (Mark 1:37–39)

Personal Walls and Gates: (1) Do you carefully assess how a new task impacts your availability? Are you willing to off-load activities and responsibilities in order to focus on the new effort? (2) Do you seek God's guidance, or do you begin based on experience or knowledge? Do you assume the experiences of the past are adequate for today? Do you assume that God wants to do things the same way today as he did in the past? (3) Do you see God's hand in your life? Do you give him the credit? (4) Have you given God control of your life, or do you have a contingency contract with him, calling on him when needed? Is God in control or just on call?

Community Walls and Gates: As others respond to God's call, do you recognize the impact on ministries when that person is no longer available? Do you assist in finding someone to fill that vacancy?

Disciples respond to God's call.

Initial Opposition

> Then I came to the governors of the province
> Beyond the River and gave them the king's
> letters. Now the king had sent with me officers
> of the army and horsemen. But when Sanballat
> the Horonite and Tobiah the Ammonite servant
> heard this, it displeased them greatly that someone
> had come to seek the welfare of the people of
> Israel. (2:9–10)

Nehemiah made a courtesy call on the governors of provinces east of the Jordan River to let them know that he was the new governor of Jerusalem and what he would be doing there. He showed them the letters of authorization from the king.

Some speculate that Sanballat and Tobiah were both governors, one in Samaria and the other in Ammon (the Trans-Jordan region).[10] Others believe they may have been senior political figures and heard about Nehemiah's presence and plan indirectly without receiving the full details as implied in Nehemiah 2:19.

While this was to be a peaceful effort, it troubled Sanballat and Tobiah that someone was meddling in the affairs of the Jews. They may have viewed the rebuilding effort as a threat to their positions.

In beginning a project, it is important to reveal your plans and the reasons for them to those that may be affected. We should not be surprised when we encounter opposition. In this case, it was external, although Tobiah's name appears to have Hebrew roots.[11]

Remember that Nehemiah had bathed this effort in months of prayer. Paul encourages us to fight our battles with prayer.

> For we do not wrestle against flesh and blood, but against the rulers, against the authorities, against the cosmic powers over this present darkness, against the spiritual forces of evil in the heavenly places. Therefore take up the whole armor of God, that you may be able to withstand in the evil day, and having done all, to stand firm. (Ephesians 6:12)

Personal Walls and Gates: Have you immerse
d your God-given task in prayer? Do you let people know what you are doing? Are you open and clear about your intentions? Are you prepared for opposition?

Community Walls and Gates: Do you come alongside others in their efforts? Are you an encourager in the face of opposition?

> **Disciples cover their efforts in prayer
> and make their plans known.**

Inspecting Walls and Gates

> So I went to Jerusalem and was there three days. Then I arose in the night, I and a few men with me. And I told no one what my God had put into my heart to do for Jerusalem. There was no animal with me but the one on which I rode. I went out by night by the Valley Gate to the Dragon

Spring and to the Dung Gate, and I inspected the walls of Jerusalem that were broken down and its gates that had been destroyed by fire. Then I went on to the Fountain Gate and to the King's Pool, but there was no room for the animal that was under me to pass. Then I went up in the night by the valley and inspected the wall, and I turned back and entered by the Valley Gate, and so returned. And the officials did not know where I had gone or what I was doing, and I had not yet told the Jews, the priests, the nobles, the officials, and the rest who were to do the work. (2:11–16).

Nehemiah started with a broad goal: rebuild the walls and gates of Jerusalem. To do that, he needed to know the scope of the effort and what was needed. He made a quiet tour of the southern walls at night to determine the extent of the task and what was needed. Some speculate that the northern walls were the most severely damaged as Jerusalem had historically been attacked from the north.[12]

He took a few men with him to survey the conditions. They were either men who came with him or men of Jerusalem whom he could trust.

When God gives us a task, it often comes in broad general terms. Like Nehemiah, we need to understand the specifics and the cost. We need to assess the situation. And like Nehemiah, we need to do it without fanfare. Jesus encourages us to count the cost.

For which of you, desiring to build a tower, does not first sit down and count the cost, whether he has enough to complete it? Otherwise, when he has laid a foundation and is not able to finish, all who see it begin to mock him. (Luke 14:28–29)

Personal Walls and Gates: Do you quietly assess the scope of a God-given task before starting? Do you engage trusted individuals in evaluating the task? Do you call men together to pray about the vision? Do you build ownership among the leadership?
Community Walls and Gates: Are you a part of the inspection team? Do you contribute to the assessment?

A disciple counts the cost.

Casting the Vision

Then I said to them, "You see the trouble we are in, how Jerusalem lies in ruins with its gates burned. Come, let us build the wall of Jerusalem, that we may no longer suffer derision." And I told them of the hand of my God that had been upon me for good, and also of the words that the king had spoken to me. And they said, "Let us rise up and build." So they strengthened their hands for the good work. (2:17–18)

Previous efforts to restore the walls had failed. The people gave up. It took Nehemiah, an "outsider," to bring fresh eyes and vision to the situation. He cast that vision to the leadership of Jerusalem.

It must have been an overwhelming vision. But Nehemiah stated that God was behind the effort and that the king had encouraged the effort. The leadership was inspired and responded with "Let us rise up and build." The need in Jerusalem was for a vision and effective leadership. Nehemiah was a dynamic, hands-on motivator.

Advancing God's kingdom requires visionaries, leaders, and followers. As disciples, our task may appear to be impossible. Yet Jesus promised that we will be empowered for the task.

> But you will receive power when the Holy Spirit has come upon you, and you will be my witnesses in Jerusalem and in all Judea and Samaria, and to the end of the earth. (Acts 1:8)

Personal Walls and Gates: Are you careful to define the vision and what it will take before you launch the effort? Do you bring the leadership in early? Are you certain that the task is God-given and that he will empower you?

Community Walls and Gates: Where do you fit? Do you cast the vision? Or do you "rise up" to build? It takes both types of people.

Disciples inspire by casting the vision.

Renewed Opposition

> But when Sanballat the Horonite and Tobiah the Ammonite servant and Geshem the Arab heard of it, they jeered at us and despised us and said, "What is this thing that you are doing? Are you rebelling against the king?" Then I replied to them, "The God of heaven will make us prosper, and we his servants will arise and build, but you

have no portion or right or claim in Jerusalem."
(2:19–20)

At this point, there were three opponents of the reconstruction project: Sanballat, Tobias, and Gesham. Geshem was believed to be a powerful overlord in northwest Arabia who operated under Persian authority.[13]

The three accused Nehemiah of rebelling against the king. They saw an opportunity to undermine Nehemiah's efforts and authority. At a minimum, they viewed a restored Jerusalem as a threat to the current political and territorial environment.

Nonetheless, Nehemiah ignored his opponents. He again stated his confidence that God would bring success to the project. Nehemiah soundly rejected any claim by the three to the city and region.

It is God who directs and brings success to our projects. We can only move forward, despite opposition, under God's power and guidance.

> Blessed are you when others revile you and persecute you and utter all kinds of evil against you falsely on my account. Rejoice and be glad, for your reward is great in heaven, for so they persecuted the prophets who were before you. (Matthew 5:11–12)

Personal Walls and Gates: Are you prepared for opposition to God's plans? Do you understand that opposition comes with the Lord's work?

Community Walls and Gates: Are you confident and discerning enough to say to opponents, "You have no part in this"?

Disciples move forward with confidence in God.

Organization, Leadership, and Laborers (Part 1)

> Then Eliashib the high priest rose up with his brothers the priests, and they built the Sheep Gate. They consecrated it and set its doors. They consecrated it as far as the Tower of the Hundred, as far as the Tower of Hananel. And next to him the men of Jericho built. And next to them Zaccur the son of Imri built ... And between the upper chamber of the corner and the Sheep Gate the goldsmiths and the merchants repaired. (3:1–32)

On the surface, chapter 3 appears to be an administrative record of who was involved in the reconstruction and where they worked. However, several spiritual principles come through.

1. The record explains that the work of rebuilding the gates and walls was divided into reasonable and achievable tasks and those tasks were assigned to identifiable groups and individuals under assigned leaders.
2. Some of the work was led by priests (3:1, 17, 22, and 28) and other work by laymen.
3. Nehemiah enlisted workers from the region, not just Jerusalem and its surroundings. For example, the men of

Jericho traveled more than a day to get to Jerusalem (3:2). The men of Tekoa (3:5) came from a town south of Bethlehem.

We are called to advance his kingdom. The Lord has given us spiritual gifts to do that. While some may have the same gift, the specific calling determines where and how that gift is to be applied.

> Now you are the body of Christ and individually members of it. And God has appointed in the church first apostles, second prophets, third teachers, then miracles, then gifts of healing, helping, administrating, and various kinds of tongues. Are all apostles? Are all prophets? Are all teachers? Do all work miracles? Do all possess gifts of healing? Do all speak with tongues? Do all interpret? But earnestly desire the higher gifts. And I will show you a still more excellent way. (1 Corinthians 12:27–30)

Personal Walls and Gates: To what section of the wall has God assigned you: missionary, pastor, church planter, youth worker, outreach, disciple-maker, small group leader, Sunday school teacher, or other? As a laborer for the Lord, what is your motivation: working with your hands, working with people, or working with your mind?

Community Walls and Gates: Are there those on the sidelines who need to be engaged in organizing and leading? Are you encouraging them?

Disciples work together to advance the kingdom of God.
Organization, Leadership, and Laborers (Part 2)

Let us continue with the spiritual principles in chapter 3.

4. Some workers labored outside their area of expertise, such as goldsmiths (3:8, 31, 32), perfume makers (3:9), leaders (3:9, 12,14, 15, 16, 18), women (3:12), temple servants and priests (3:17,22, 28), and merchants (3:32).

We are experts at making excuses. "I do not have the skills." "It is not my spiritual gift or skills." "I could be injured." "I don't have time." "I'm busy doing something else for the Lord."

5. As indicated earlier, the northern section was rubble. Therefore, the workers had to build the wall (3:3), not repair it.

Some are called to build, and others to restore. Regardless, the objective is the same: a healthy, vibrant, effective fellowship under the Lord.

6. Some nobles considered the work to be beneath them and refused to work under supervision (v. 5).

Advancing the kingdom is an "all-hands-on-deck" effort. The Lord calls all to advance his kingdom. He has called us to advance his kingdom regardless of skill or position.

> For you were called to freedom, brothers. Only do not use your freedom as an opportunity for the flesh, but through love serve one another. (Galatians 5:13)

Personal Walls and Gates: (1) Are you willing to step out of your comfort zone to serve the Lord? Are you willing to take risks for the Lord? (2) Are you willing to serve where someone has assigned you? (3) When God calls, do you check to see if it is compatible with your perceived position? Do you approach the task with humility? Are you concerned about how people might see you?

Community Walls and Gates: Do you encourage those in your fellowship to engage in the work? Do you offer to work alongside of them? Do you share how their skills can be used?

Disciples grow where they are planted.

Withstanding Ridicule

> Now when Sanballat heard that we were building the wall, he was angry and greatly enraged, and he jeered at the Jews. And he said in the presence of his brothers and of the army of Samaria, "What are these feeble Jews doing? Will they restore it for themselves? Will they sacrifice? Will they finish up in a day? Will they revive the stones out of the heaps of rubbish, and burned ones at that?" Tobiah the Ammonite was beside him, and he said, "Yes, what they are building— if a fox goes up on it he will break down their stone wall!" (4:1–3)

Sanballat and Tobiah increased their ridcule. They apparently observed Nehemiah's organizational and leadership skills and saw the rebuilding effort taking shape. The reference to sacrifices implies that they would call on God to help them.

There is no reference in Nehemiah that stones were being quarried; therefore, the builders were using what was available in the rubble, even stones burned in the destruction of the city in 586 BC. Sanballat and Tobiah taunted the workers. Their attacks were verbal.

Hurtful words can be discouraging. Today our culture ridicules those with whom they disagree, particularly believers. We have been described as those who "hold onto their guns and Bibles." In our culture, it is all right to talk to God, but if God answers, you have a serious problem.

The adage "Sticks and stones may break my bones, but names will never harm me" is false. Broken bones heal, but people may carry hurtful words into life with harmful effects.

When we are obedient in a God-given task and are ridiculed, and we will, we should understand that the ridicule is directed toward God.

> But rejoice insofar as you share Christ's sufferings, that you may also rejoice and be glad when his glory is revealed. (1 Peter 4:13)

Personal Walls and Gates: Have you been or are you the subject of ridicule? What is or was your response? Can you, with the Lord's help, set it aside? Do you have a forgiving spirit?

Community Walls and Gates: Do you know someone who is or has been ridiculed? Are you bearing that burden with them? Are you an encourager?

A disciple understands the target of ridicule.

Nehemiah's Prayer

> Hear, O our God, for we are despised; turn their reproach on their own heads and give them as plunder to a land of captivity! Do not cover their iniquity, and do not let their sin be blotted out from before You; for they have provoked *You* to anger before the builders. (4:4–5)

Nehemiah's response to strong ridicule was to go to prayer. This is the first of eight brief prayers. It was not a quick request for help. Rather, it was an impassioned plea. He tells God something he already knew: the opposition is not worthy of his attention. It was important for Nehemiah (and the builders) to recognize that they were operating according to God's plan. The opposition was outside the will of God. Nehemiah's prayer was not a prayer for vengeance. It was a prayer recognizing the future of those who oppose God and his plans. It was recognition that the opposition was against God himself. The opposition was dishonoring God.

Praying in the face of opposition is not a normal human response. Ridicule usually brings up anger and thoughts of vengeance. How we react to opposition is a testimony to our relationship with the Lord. From a New Testament perspective, in our prayers we need to apply Nehemiah's faith that God will bring justice to an unjust world. Paul teaches us to be in prayer continually.

> Rejoice always, pray without ceasing, give thanks in all circumstances; for this is the will of God in Christ Jesus for you. (1 Thessalonians 5:16–17)

Personal Walls and Gates: Do you bathe your efforts in prayer? Do you understand that pursuing a God-given task is a threat to Satan? Even in Satan's death throes, he opposes our efforts in advancing the kingdom. Do we *know* that we are engaged in spiritual warfare?

Community Walls and Gates: Is there someone in your circle of friends who is facing opposition? Do they know you are there for them? Do they know God is there for them?

Disciples pray in the face of opposition.

CONSTRUCTING THE WALLS

Progressing Together

> So we built the wall, and the entire wall was
> joined together up to half its *height,* for the people
> had a mind to work. (4:6)

There are three points here. First, the people responded
positively to strong, impassioned, and organized leadership. The
work progressed despite verbal assaults.

Second, everyone came together on the effort. The people
were unified. They gave serious attention to the work.

Third, there was a visual indicator of progress. The gaps in
the wall had been filled, and the wall had been raised to half its
planned height. This was despite the northern section being
nothing but rubble at the start. Identifiable progress motivates
effort.

It would be safe to credit the progress to Nehemiah's
leadership. On the other hand, the commitment of the people

was due to their faith in God. It was God who inspired the work just as Paul claimed in Acts.

> And now, behold, I am going to Jerusalem, constrained by the Spirit, not knowing what will happen to me there, except that the Holy Spirit testifies to me in every city that imprisonment and afflictions await me. But I do not account my life of any value nor as precious to myself, if only I may finish my course and the ministry that I received from the Lord Jesus, to testify to the gospel of the grace of God. (Acts 20:22–24)

Personal Walls and Gates: Do you have a clear picture of the finished product? Have you identified measurable, intermediate steps in your plan?

Community Walls and Gates: Do those engaged in the effort have a clear understanding of the finished product? Do you keep them informed on progress?

Disciples work together to achieve the objective.

More Opposition

> But when Sanballat and Tobiah and the Arabs and the Ammonites and the Ashdodites heard that the repairing of the walls of Jerusalem was going forward and that the breaches were beginning to be closed, they were very angry. And they all plotted together to come and fight against Jerusalem and to cause confusion in it. And we

prayed to our God and set a guard as a
protection against them day and night. (4:7–9)

The opposition assumed that the effort could be halted with
contempt and ridicule (4:1–3). When that failed, they plotted
active intervention. Notice that the response of the opposition
was based on what they heard, not actual observation. Brennen
points out that the four opposing groups came from the north,
south, east, and west, literally surrounding the city.[14]

The workers responded in two ways: they prayed and kept an
eye out for the enemy.

Satan uses numerous tactics to discourage and hinder God's
work. As in Nehemiah's day, the opposition comes from all
directions. Building our faith means developing spiritual barriers
to the world, the flesh, and the devil. Satan uses the attractions
of our past life to distract us. The temptation to descend into
disobedience is very real. We need gates designed to let the
Spirit direct through the Word, prayer, and fellowship.

Satan opposes work to advance the kingdom in various
forms: resistance from the community, government authorities,
businesses, and individuals who oppose the gospel or do not
understand the work as mentioned by Paul in 1 Thessalonians.

> You know, brothers, that our visit to you was not
> a failure. We had previously suffered and been
> insulted in Philippi, as you know, but with the
> help of our God we dared to tell you his gospel in
> spite of strong opposition. (1 Thessalonians 2:1–2
> NKJV)

Personal Walls and Gates: Are you struggling against the world, the flesh, or the devil? Are outside forces actively opposing your efforts to advance the gospel? Are you responding in prayer?

Community Walls and Gates: Who in your sphere of influence is under perceived or real attack? Are you coming alongside them in prayer? Are you bringing others into the arena of prayer?

Disciples bring prayer to bear on opposition.

The Enemy's Threats

> In Judah it was said, "The strength of those who bear the burdens is failing. There is too much rubble. By ourselves we will not be able to rebuild the wall." And our enemies said, "They will not know or see till we come among them and kill them and stop the work." At that time the Jews who lived near them came from all directions and said to us ten times, "You must return to us." (4:10–12)

The workers were discouraged and stopped working (4:15). They were exhausted, the task was difficult, and they were under threat from every direction. It appears that families of the workers encouraged them to return home to avoid the expected battle. There were both internal and external threats.

Why is it that when there is progress in the Lord's work, challenges arise? As with the repair of the walls and gates, things never seem to progress fast enough, the work appears to be beyond our capability, and there are those who actively oppose the work. The psalmist's response to such situations was this: "Unless the Lord builds the house, they labor in vain who build it" (Psalm 127:1). Paul reminded the Galatians not to give up.

> It is the Lord who instills vision, motivates the workers, and provides protection. And let us not grow weary of doing good, for in due season we will reap, if we do not give up. (Galatians 6:9)

Personal Walls and Gates: Are you growing weary in serving the Lord? Do you take obstacles and opposition personally? Are you bathing the effort in prayer?

Community Walls and Gates: Are you a source of encouragement for others in the battle? Do you make yourself available to assist the effort? Do you help them see the real source of opposition?

Disciples do not grow weary in the face of opposition.

Guarding the Effort

> So in the lowest parts of the space behind the wall, in open places, I stationed the people by their clans, with their swords, their spears, and their bows. And I looked and arose and said to the nobles and to the officials and to the rest of the people, "Do not be afraid of them. Remember the Lord, who is great and awesome, and fight for your brothers, your sons, your daughters, your wives, and your homes." (4:13–14)

The work come to a halt as a result of the threats from five groups (4:7). Nehemiah was not discouraged. He knew the size of the task and the strength of the opposition. He organized the people for defense, posted them at the weakest points, and reminded them that God would fight for them. While God was beside them, they needed to be prepared should an attack occur.

Attacks against the work of the Lord is spiritual warfare. The most powerful weapon we have is prayer. Through prayer, the Lord will provide guidance on meeting challenges or will change the situation as taught by Paul in Philippians.

> Brothers, I do not consider that I have made it my own. But one thing I do: forgetting what lies behind and straining forward to what lies ahead, I press on toward the goal for the prize of the upward call of God in Christ Jesus. (Philippians 3:13–14)

Personal Walls and Gates: Do you become discouraged when things do not go the way you planned? Or like Nehemiah, do you place the situation before the Lord? How great is your God?
Community Walls and Gates: Do you encourage one another when the going gets rough? Do you engage in prayer for others being challenged?

Disciples press on.

Swords for Defense

> When our enemies heard that it was known to us and that God had frustrated their plan, we all

returned to the wall, each to his work. From that day on, half of my servants worked on construction, and half held the spears, shields, bows, and coats of mail. And the leaders stood behind the whole house of Judah, who were building on the wall. Those who carried burdens were loaded in such a way that each labored on the work with one hand and held his weapon with the other. And each of the builders had his sword strapped at his side while he built. The man who sounded the trumpet was beside me. (4:15–18)

The work stopped in the face of internal and external opposition. Nehemiah divided the workforce into guards and laborers. All the workers were armed, not just the guards. There was a job for everyone. Some set stones (pastors, teachers, evangelists, and prophets). Others carried materials (helps, mercy, hospitality, and encouragers). Others guarded (prayer warriors and intercessors). And there were the trumpeters (discernment).

Now there are varieties of gifts, but the same Spirit; and there are varieties of service, but the same Lord; and there are varieties of activities, but it is the same God who empowers them all in everyone. To each is given the manifestation of the Spirit for the common good. (1 Corinthians 12:4–7)

Personal Walls and Gates: What is your role in advancing the kingdom? As a leader, have you organized the work according to spiritual gifts? Are you laboring under the guidance and direction of a leader?

Community Walls and Gates: Are you helping others determine their role?

Disciples work together employing their gifts uniquely.

Vigilance is Needed

> And I said to the nobles and to the officials and to the rest of the people, "The work is great and widely spread, and we are separated on the wall, far from one another. In the place where you hear the sound of the trumpet, rally to us there. Our God will fight for us." (4:19–20)

Some early manuscripts of the narrative suggest that there were multiple trumpeters. Josephus, a first-century Jewish historian, suggests that Nehemiah placed trumpeters five hundred feet apart throughout the work with a single trumpeter to start the alarm.[15]

Nehemiah was preparing for a "holy war" because he was carrying out God's plan, and he was confident that God would fight for his people.

Today, while we do not have trumpeters beside us, we have the Word, prayer, and each other to warn of attacks. We also have the Holy Spirit who will alert us, stand by us, and defend us.

> For though we walk in the flesh, we are not waging war according to the flesh. For the weapons of our warfare are not of the flesh but have divine power to destroy strongholds. We destroy arguments and every lofty opinion raised against the knowledge of God, and take every thought captive to obey Christ, being ready to punish every disobedience, when your obedience is complete. (2 Corinthians 10:3–5)

Personal Walls and Gates: Do you have a routine time in the Word and prayer? Do you have an accountability partner? Have you experienced the Holy Spirit's power in combating the attacks of Satan?

Community Walls and Gates: Are you vigilant in warning others of imminent attack? Do you stand with others who are under attack?

Disciples have an effective alert system.

Bring a Sense of Urgency

> So we labored at the work, and half of them held the spears from the break of dawn until the stars came out. I also said to the people at that time, "Let every man and his servant pass the night within Jerusalem, that they may be a guard for us by night and may labor by day." So neither I nor my brothers nor my servants nor the men of the guard who followed me, none of us took off our clothes; each kept his weapon at his right hand. (4:21–23)

There is a sense of urgency in these verses. There was a need for protection from expected attacks from Sanballat and his allies. Moreover, completion of the walls and gates would give them security. Because families were encouraging workers to leave the work and return home, Nehemiah kept the workers in the city at night. Under Nehemiah's direction, the workers were protected, and the work continued.

In advancing Christ's kingdom, there must be a sense of urgency. We need to be prepared for attacks from the enemy. Prayer warriors with the Word in hand need to be in place. Work on our personal and community walls and gates is a continuing process.

> Then they were on the road. They preached with joyful urgency that life can be radically different; right and left they sent the demons packing; they brought wellness to the sick, anointing their bodies, healing their spirits. (Mark 6:12–13 MSG)

Personal Walls and Gates: Do you have a sense of urgency in building personal walls and gates? Are you building walls and gates for your family and for your work?

Community Walls and Gates: Do those around you have a sense of urgency in advancing the kingdom? Are you an encourager? Are you an exhorter?

Disciples advance the kingdom with a sense of urgency.

Internal Strife

Now there arose a great outcry of the people and of their wives against their Jewish brothers. For there were those who said, "With our sons and our daughters, we are many. So let us get grain, that we may eat and keep alive." There were also those who said, "We are mortgaging our fields, our vineyards, and our houses to get grain because of the famine." And there were those who said, "We have borrowed money for the king's tax on our fields and our vineyards. Now our flesh is as the flesh of our brothers, our children are as their children. Yet we are forcing our sons and our daughters to be slaves, and some of our daughters have already been enslaved, but it is not in our power to help it, for other men have our fields and our vineyards." (5:1–5)

Nehemiah had just established a way of guarding against an attack by external opposition. The work on the walls and gates resumed. Then another issue arose requiring his attention. Some scholars speculate that the rebuilding project further stressed the people who were already burdened by an economic crisis.[16] The tipping point may have been the decision to keep the workers in the city where they could not work the fields. They had no income. Moreover, Artaxerxes had not suspended taxation.[17]

The crisis was created by a famine. As a result, there was a lack of food among the landless, landowners had mortgaged their lands to buy food, others had to take out loans at high rates of interest to pay taxes, and still others were forced to sell themselves and children into slavery to survive.

Clearly the situation had been building for some time, and no one had stepped up to deal with it.

Why is it that when undertaking a major effort for the Lord, something significant comes up that needs immediate attention?

> Now in these days when the disciples were increasing in number, a complaint by the Hellenists arose against the Hebrews because their widows were being neglected in the daily distribution. And the twelve summoned the full number of the disciples and said, "It is not right that we should give up preaching the word of God to serve tables. (Acts 6:1–2)

Personal Walls and Gates: How do you respond when things interfere with your well-laid plans? Is it with anger? With frustration? Do you call a halt and address the situation?

Community Walls and Gates: In your situation, what needs are pressing and must be met? Who are the disadvantaged that need help?

Disciples are sensitive to the needs of others.

Nehemiah's Response to the Outcry

> I was very angry when I heard their outcry and these words. I took counsel with myself, and I brought charges against the nobles and the officials. I said to them, "You are exacting interest, each from his brother." And I held a

great assembly against them and said to them, "We, as far as we are able, have bought back our Jewish brothers who have been sold to the nations, but you even sell your brothers that they may be sold to us!" They were silent and could not find a word to say. (5:6–8)

Nehemiah was angry with the nobility and rulers over the way they were treating their poorer brethren. He may also have been angry at himself for being so focused on rebuilding the walls and gates that he had overlooked the injustice.

Nehemiah stopped to address the issue. He did not put the matter on hold. He took time to let his anger cool and to consider how to respond to the issues.

Nehemiah was quick to recognize who was responsible for the injustice. He addressed those responsible in open forum by arguing from a historical context—the exile of the Israelites. He accused the leaders of selling the people into slavery.

The guilt of the nobles and rulers was so heavy they had nothing to say. The writer of the book of Acts set criteria for leaders when complaints arose about the needs of widows not being met.

Therefore, brothers, pick out from among you seven men of good repute, full of the Spirit and of wisdom, whom we will appoint to this duty. (Acts 6:3)

Personal Walls and Gates: How do you respond to injustice? Does it make you angry? Do you put it off for a more convenient time? Do you think about where you can be involved? What might be your role in solving the problem?

Community Walls and Gates: Where do you see injustice in your community?

Disciples are angered by injustice.

The Root of the Problem

> So I said, "The thing that you are doing is not good. Ought you not to walk in the fear of our God to prevent the taunts of the nations our enemies? Moreover, I and my brothers and my servants are lending them money and grain. Let us abandon this exacting of interest. Return to them this very day their fields, their vineyards, their olive orchards, and their houses, and the percentage of money, grain, wine, and oil that you have been exacting from them." (5:9–11)

A responsibility of leadership is to lighten the load on the people. The Law called for leaders to use their power and influence to reduce, if not eliminate, injustice. Leaders should act for the powerless.

Nehemiah understood the Law. He asked the nobility and rulers how they were perceived by outsiders. Why are you doing this to your brothers? Think about how others view your actions.

Gaining profit or loaning money was not prohibited by the Law.

But the Law was clear: greed was a sin.

Nehemiah directed the nobility and rulers to restore what

they had taken with interest. (Some interpret the words "a hundredth" to mean 1 percent per month.)[18]

Lending without usury was an act of kindness. Nehemiah was exhorting the leaders to stop pressing claims on loans.

Although he was not a participant in this injustice, he set the example. He and his associates took personal action to correct the situation.

> "So whatever you wish that others would do to you, do also to them, for this is the Law and the Prophets." (Matthew 7:12)

Personal Walls and Gates: Are you taking the lead against injustice in your situation? Are you engaged in righting a wrong? **Community Walls and Gates:** What types of injustice do you see around you? What can you do about it?

Disciples undertake for the powerless.

Restoration

> Then they said, "We will restore these and require nothing from them. We will do as you say." And I called the priests and made them swear to do as they had promised. I also shook out the fold of my garment and said, "So may God shake out every man from his house and from his labor who does not keep this promise. So may he be shaken out and emptied." And all the assembly said "Amen" and praised the LORD. And the people did as they had promised. (5:12–13)

The nobility and rulers stopped their unlawful activities. Furthermore, Nehemiah established accountability through the religious leaders; the priests were to oversee the restoration.

Nehemiah shook out his robe (sash or pockets) as a visual indication of accountability before God. In that culture, it was a ritual act expressing the seriousness of the oath being taken. Some suggest that the folds of a robe were an illustration of rooms in a house and asking God to evict the disobedient.[19]

The leaders responded with "Amen," a verbal expression of their commitment to restore the wrong.

Clearly the people had reached a breaking point. Some speculate that if the injustice had been allowed to continue, the unrest could have escalated and achieved what Sanballat and Tobiah had been threatening. However, Nehemiah's quick action met the need and allowed work on the walls and gates to continue.

Paul warned the Galatians that sin interferes with the work of the Lord.

> Brothers, if anyone is caught in any transgression, you who are spiritual should restore him in a spirit of gentleness. Keep watch on yourself, lest you too be tempted. (Galatians 6:1)

Personal Walls and Gates: How do you restore those who have failed to live out their faith: with anger or gentleness? Do you move quickly to right wrongs?

Community Walls and Gates: Is their accountability among your leadership?

A disciple restores injustice with gentleness.

Nehemiah's Example

> Moreover, from the time that I was appointed to be their governor in the land of Judah, from the twentieth year to the thirty-second year of Artaxerxes the king, twelve years, neither I nor my brothers ate the food allowance of the governor. The former governors who were before me laid heavy burdens on the people and took from them for their daily ration forty shekels of silver. Even their servants lorded it over the people. But I did not do so, because of the fear of God. I also persevered in the work on this wall, and we acquired no land, and all my servants were gathered there for the work. (5:14–16)

Nehemiah reported that it was his policy not to take more from the people than the allowance permitted governors. That allowance covered not only his personal needs but also the needs of his servants. It was his intent to live within his budget. He did not enrich himself at the expense of the people. He did not burden the people. In living by this principle, he was able to call the nobility and rulers into accountability.

Moreover, neither he nor his servants bought land. In other words, they did not enrich themselves with property because of their positions. He and his staff did not seek personal enrichment or gain from the time he was appointed governor.

He stated that he lived by these policies out of respect for God's Law and compassion for the people.

Nehemiah was an example of servant-leadership. He worked alongside the people and had compassion for them. Likewise, Paul was not a burden on the people with whom he worked.

> After this Paul left Athens and went to Corinth. And he found a Jew named Aquila, a native of Pontus, recently come from Italy with his wife Priscilla, because Claudius had commanded all the Jews to leave Rome. And he went to see them, and because he was of the same trade he stayed with them and worked, for they were tentmakers by trade. And he reasoned in the synagogue every Sabbath, and tried to persuade Jews and Greeks. (Acts 18:1–4)

Personal Walls and Gates: Do you insist on your rights? Do you assume that the power, authority, and resources available to you are yours? Do you understand, at the action level, that God expects you to apply the resources he has given you with love and compassion?

Community Walls and Gates: What needs do you see around you? How can you and your fellow believers help meet those needs?

A disciple is a living testimony.

Nehemiah's Sacrifice

> Moreover, there were at my table 150 men, Jews and officials, besides those who came to us from the nations that were around us. Now what was

prepared at my expense for each day was one ox and six choice sheep and birds, and every ten days all kinds of wine in abundance. Yet for all this I did not demand the food allowance of the governor, because the service was too heavy on this people. Remember for my good, O my God, all that I have done for this people. (5:17–19)

Nehemiah continued to stress his concern for the people by describing his social responsibilities as governor. Some believe that Nehemiah included poorer members of society in these festive occasions. He did not dip into the governor's allowance or demand provisions from the people.
Mathew Henry speculates that Nehemiah funded these extravagant affairs out of his own pocket—from savings accumulated from his time in the court of Artaxerxes or from his estate in Judah.[20]

I appeal to you therefore, brothers, by the mercies of God, to present your bodies as a living sacrifice, holy and acceptable to God, which is your spiritual worship. Do not be conformed to this world, but be transformed by the renewal of your mind, that by testing you may discern what is the will of God, what is good and acceptable and perfect. (Romans 12:1–2)

Personal Walls and Gates: What does it mean to sacrifice? Does it mean your time? Is it in terms of possessions or money? How is your sacrifice related to tithes and offerings?

Community Walls and Gates: Where are you being called to sacrifice?

A disciple sacrifices for the Lord.

Confronting Evil

> Now when Sanballat and Tobiah and Geshem the Arab and the rest of our enemies heard that I had built the wall and that there was no breach left in it (although up to that time I had not set up the doors in the gates), Sanballat and Geshem sent to me, saying, "Come and let us meet together at Hakkephirim in the plain of Ono." But they intended to do me harm. And I sent messengers to them, saying, "I am doing a great work and I cannot come down. Why should the work stop while I leave it and come down to you?" And they sent to me four times in this way, and I answered them in the same manner. (6:1–4)

Sanballat, Tobiah, and Geshem's earlier charges were an attempt to stop the work on the walls and gates. This attempt was directly against Nehemiah. Having been unsuccessful in stopping the work, they then launched a personal attack.

One could read into the invitation as a call to negotiation, if not peace. Nehemiah saw through the request as an attempt to distract him, if not to kill him. Certainly, he distrusted the three. On the other hand, his discernment came from his relationship with the Lord. He understood that if he were to be removed from the work, it would stop.

Walls and gates are visible signs of strength. They are inflexible and pose a significant challenge to the opposition (the world).

The enemy is persistent in opposition and deception. Like Nehemiah, we must be discerning, focused, and determined to keep our personal walls and gates in good repair.

> "I know your works, your toil and your patient endurance, and how you cannot bear with those who are evil but have tested those who call themselves apostles and are not and found them to be false. I know you are enduring patiently and bearing up for my name's sake, and you have not grown weary." (Revelation 2:2–3)

Personal Walls and Gates: Are you aware of the enemy's opposition and ways he can interfere? Does your life pose a challenge to the world?

Community Walls and Gates: Who in your sphere of influence needs encouragement in the battle?

Disciples are persistent in the face of opposition.

The Enemy's Accusations

> In the same way Sanballat for the fifth time sent his servant to me with an open letter in his hand. In it was written, "It is reported among the nations, and Geshem also says it, that you and the Jews intend to rebel; that is why you are building

the wall. And according to these reports you wish to become their king. And you have also set up prophets to proclaim concerning you in Jerusalem, 'There is a king in Judah.' And now the king will hear of these reports. So now come and let us take counsel together." (6:5–7)

Having failed in previous attempts to stop the work on the walls and gates, Sanballat escalated the opposition by accusing Nehemiah of attempting to establish a kingdom in Judah.

Moreover, he accused Nehemiah of enlisting false prophets to elevate him in the eyes of the people. He threatened to inform Artaxerxes of the "threat" to his kingdom. Sanballat misrepresented Nehemiah's intent and attempted to intimidate the leaders, workers, and people with his open letter.

This is a clear picture of Satan's attacks on our efforts to advance Christ's kingdom. He uses intimidation, insinuation, and false accusations to discourage, demoralize, and disrupt the work of the Lord.

For the one who sows to his own flesh will from the flesh reap corruption, but the one who sows to the Spirit will from the Spirit reap eternal life. And let us not grow weary of doing good, for in due season we will reap, if we do not give up. So then, as we have opportunity, let us do good to everyone, and especially to those who are of the household of faith. (Galatians 6:8–10)

Personal Walls and Gates: Do you grow weary and lose strength under attacks on your God-given efforts? Are you working in your own wisdom and strength?

Community Walls and Gates: Do you come along side of those under attack? Do you keep them in your prayers? Do they know you are standing with them?

Disciples do not take threats to obedience personally.

Nehemiah's Response

> Then I sent to him, saying, "No such things as you say have been done, for you are inventing them out of your own mind." For they all wanted to frighten us, thinking, "Their hands will drop from the work, and it will not be done." But now, O God, strengthen my hands. (6:8–9)

Nehemiah's response to Sanballat's charges was blunt. He stated that Sanballat's accusations were his own invention and baseless. Nehemiah recognized that the claims were an attempt to demoralize the people and stop the rebuilding. Nehemiah was determined to continue the work.

Many scholars view the words "O God, strengthen my hands" as a prayer. Some ancient texts translate these words as "So now I increased my efforts."[21] Satan actively opposes God's work. He will use anything to stop the work. Our response must be clear—we are empowered by the Holy Spirit. God is with us. Therefore, we cannot fail.

But though we had already suffered and been shamefully treated at Philippi, as you know, we had boldness in our God to declare to you the gospel of God during much conflict. (1 Thessalonians 2:2)

Personal Walls and Gates: How do you respond to opposition? Is it based on the knowledge that God will carry the effort through? Do you operate under the power of Jesus's name?

Community Walls and Gates: Who in your community is under attack? Do you come alongside them to "hold up their arms" so their efforts prevail?

Disciples understand there will be opposition to the Lord's work.

The Conspiracy

Now when I went into the house of Shemaiah the son of Delaiah, son of Mehetabel, who was confined to his home, he said, "Let us meet together in the house of God, within the temple. Let us close the doors of the temple, for they are coming to kill you. They are coming to kill you by night." But I said, "Should such a man as I run away? And what man such as I could go into the temple and live? I will not go in." And I understood and saw that God had not sent him, but he had pronounced the prophecy against me because Tobiah and Sanballat had hired him. For this purpose he was hired, that I should be afraid and act in this way and sin, and so they could give me a bad name in order to taunt me. Remember Tobiah and Sanballat, O my God, according to these things that they did, and also the prophetess Noadiah and the rest of the prophets who wanted to make me afraid. (6:10–14)

Some speculate that Shemaiah was a priest.[22] The NKJV translates Shemaiah's status as being a secret informer.[23] Getz thinks that Nehemiah considered Shemaiah to be a prophet.[24] In any case, Nehemiah met with him at his house.

There were two problems with Shemaiah's suggestion that he and Nehemiah go into the temple. First, the Hebrew text implies that they should enter the sanctuary where only priests were allowed. Second, Nehemiah would have been removed from leading the rebuilding effort. But Nehemiah refused. He understood the suggestion to be from Sanballat and Tobiah. Again, he went to prayer.

The normal reaction to this type of ruse is to flee, to take cover, and to seek safety. However, we are called to be in the world and stand in the face of opposition. Nehemiah saw taking refuge in the temple, for whatever reason, a sin.

Be watchful, stand firm in the faith, act like men, be strong. (1 Corinthians 16:13)

Personal Walls and Gates: How do you respond to the temptation to take cover in the face of opposition? Do you stand firm in the gospel? Do you bathe your response in prayer?

Community Walls and Gates: Who do you need to encourage to stand firm in the face of opposition?

A disciple stands firm in the faith.

The Walls Were Completed

> So the wall was finished on the twenty-fifth day
> of the month Elul, in fifty-two days. And when all
> our enemies heard of it, all the nations around us
> were afraid and fell greatly in their own esteem,
> for they perceived that this work had been
> accomplished with the help of our God. (6:15–16)

The walls and gates were completed in fifty-two days. The short period for rebuilding is supported by the circuit of the walls being much smaller than today and the stones were rough-hewn and not dressed as they appear today.[25] Note that Nehemiah gave the credit to the Lord.

Figure 2: Nehemiah's Wall

The walls had lain in disrepair for 142 years. It was under the motivated leadership of Nehemiah that they were restored so quickly. The completed walls and gates were a sign of strength and protection. As such, the opposition was demoralized, so much so that they also gave God the credit.

Figure 3: Water Gate Excavation

God is always at work. We see him in the success of our efforts and in the lives of those around us. When we see lives restored, spiritual transformation, miraculous protection, and healing, people recognize God's presence and power. When God's power is evident, men either acknowledge him or see him as a threat to their plans.

> And as they were speaking to the people, the priests and the captain of the temple and the Sadducees came upon them, greatly annoyed because they were teaching the people and proclaiming in Jesus the resurrection from the dead. And they arrested them and put them in custody until the next day, for it was already evening. But many of those who had heard the word believed, and the number of the men came to about five thousand. (Acts 4:1–4)

Personal Walls and Gates: What is your response to the power of God: fear or submission?

Community Walls and Gates: When you see God at work in the lives of others, do you respond with encouragement and the gospel message?

Disciples point to the power of God.

Collusion among the Enemies

> Moreover, in those days the nobles of Judah sent many letters to Tobiah, and Tobiah's letters came to them. For many in Judah were bound by oath to him, because he was the son-in-law of Shecaniah the son of Arah: and his son Jehohanan had taken the daughter of Meshullam the son of Berechiah as his wife. Also they spoke of his good deeds in my presence and reported my words to him. And Tobiah sent letters to make me afraid. (6:17–19)

These verses make it clear why the opposition was so well informed about the progress of the effort. Tobiah was not only a political power in the region, he was related to prominent families in Judah. They were "pledged" to him through marriage. They communicated with each other to undermine Nehemiah's leadership. Nehemiah was a threat to the regional power structure. To convince Nehemiah that Tobiah was of good character, the families gave good reports about him.

There are those in the world who depend on their good deeds to gain access to the kingdom of God. Good deeds are measured against the source: human effort or Spirit led.

"Not everyone who says to me, 'Lord, Lord,' will enter the kingdom of heaven, but the one who does the will of my Father who is in heaven. On that day many will say to me, 'Lord, Lord, did we not prophesy in your name, and cast out demons in your name, and do many mighty works in your name?' And then will I declare to them, 'I never knew you; depart from me, you workers of lawlessness.'" (Matthew 7:21–23)

Personal Walls and Gates: What motivates and empowers your good deeds? Do you seek to be elevated in the eyes of men or to glorify God?

Community Walls and Gates: Are you building a relationship with those who assume that "good works" will gain them access to the kingdom of God? Are you aware of people around you who believe that God grades on the curve?

Disciples live to glorify God, not themselves.

POPULATING THE CITY

Establishing Order

Now when the wall had been built and I had set up the doors, and the gatekeepers, the singers, and the Levites had been appointed, I gave my brother Hanani and Hananiah the governor of the castle charge over Jerusalem, for he was a more faithful and God-fearing man than many. And I said to them, "Let not the gates of Jerusalem be opened until the sun is hot. And while they are still standing guard, let them shut and bar the doors. Appoint guards from among the inhabitants of Jerusalem, some at their guard posts and some in front of their own homes." The city was wide and large, but the people within it were few, and no houses had been rebuilt. (7:1–4)

These verses are about the physical and spiritual protection of the city. The gatekeepers, singers, and Levites had temple responsibilities. Breneman and Holman believe Nehemiah assigned them to guard the city gates.[26] Kidner, on the other hand, believes Nehemiah's intent was reestablishing both physical and spiritual order. [27]

Nehemiah appointed his brother and another man to oversee the protection of the city. He gave them instructions on the hours that the gates were to be open. Usually city gates were opened at sunrise and closed at sunset. Some believe that the gates were closed during the heat of the day.[28]

Nehemiah brought order to the protection of the city. We also must bring order to our lives and the health of the church. Are there vulnerable places in our lives and in the church?

The Lord may call us to tasks that are outside our normal duties or not in our gifting. As in this case, we need to work together as the body of Christ, knowing that the Lord will carry us through.

> Be watchful, stand firm in the faith, act like men,
> be strong. (1 Corinthians 16:13)

Personal Walls and Gates: Is there a sense of urgency in securing and guarding the gates of your life? Are you in a mutually agreed-upon accountability relationship?

Community Walls and Gates: What gates in the church need to be guarded? Who do you allow into positions of leadership? Do people of influence in the body reflect Christ?

Disciples are called to guard the faith.

Registration of the People

> The city was wide and large, but the people within it were few, and no houses had been rebuilt. Then my God put it into my heart to assemble the nobles and the officials and the people to be enrolled by genealogy. And I found the book of the genealogy of those who came up at the first, and I found written in it. (7:4–5)

Few of those returning from Babylon were from Jerusalem because many residents were killed during the Babylonian sieges of 599 and 587 BC. Those returning from exile were mostly from outlying parts of Judah.

Moreover, those from the villages needed the protection of the walled city and, on the other hand, people were needed to help defend the city. Before Nehemiah could exercise his plan by casting lots to populate the city (11:1), he took a census to determine the heritage of those outside the city (i.e., those who could be trusted).

Furthermore, the people came to Jerusalem to worship in the temple but returned to their villages at the end of the day.

Challenge One: We need, as did Nehemiah, to have our spiritual ears tuned to God's frequency. As believers, the Holy Spirit dwells in us and we must give him control and act under his direction.

Challenge Two: We are called to bring in those who are outside the kingdom of God: those not afforded the protection of the crucified Christ. Furthermore, we need to distinguish between those who are receptive to the gospel and those who are not.

Challenge Three: As believers, we are called to be Christ to the world daily, not just on Sunday. Our success is not our own but the Lord's.

> But you will receive power when the Holy Spirit has come upon you, and you will be my witnesses in Jerusalem and in all Judea and Samaria, and to the end of the earth. (Acts 1:8)

Personal Walls and Gates: Are you inside the kingdom? Do you *know* that you are empowered to reach the lost? Do you have an intentional plan for reaching those who are receptive? Do you put God in a "Sunday box"? Do you return to your comfort zone the rest of the week? Where have you settled: inside or outside?

Community Walls and Gates: Does your community of believers have an effective, ongoing plan to reach the lost? Do you have a plan for encouraging the "Sunday only" crowd to a deeper faith?

Disciples are empowered to reach the lost.

The Record of Returnees

> These were the people of the province who came up out of the captivity of those exiles whom Nebuchadnezzar the king of Babylon had carried into exile. They returned to Jerusalem and Judah, each to his town. (7:6–63)

This chapter lists about 135 clans or groups returning to Judah. Commentators have divided the list into the following categories:[29]

- Families (7:6–25).
- Villagers (7:26–38).
- Priests (7:39–42).
- Levites (7:43–60)
- Individuals of questionable heritage (7:61–65).
- Totals (7:66–69).

Nehemiah's census was based on genealogy. Genealogies in scripture were important for several reasons.[30]

1. They confirm the reliability of the Bible.
2. They establish the importance of family to God.
3. They were important in establishing roles, responsibilities, and property rights.
4. They were important in proving prophecies.
5. And they demonstrate how God uses a wide diversity of individuals throughout history.

There are three categories of people listed: those from the tribe of Judah, the Levites, and the Nethinim. The Nethinim were servants David gave to the Levites. It is believed that they were originally Gibeanites who associated with Israel by deception (Joshua 9).

It was important for the Jews to trace the lineage of the coming Messiah. However, on this side of the cross, we can trace our spiritual heritage only to God our Father. We are a part of his family. God has no grandchildren.

So all the generations from Abraham to David were fourteen generations, and from David to the deportation to Babylon fourteen generations, and from the deportation to Babylon to the Christ fourteen generations. (Matthew 1:17)

Personal Walls and Gates: What is your spiritual heritage? Do you have assurance that you are a part of the family of God? **Community Walls and Gates:** Is leading others to the family of God a part of your DNA?

Disciples know their spiritual heritage.

Establishing Lineage

These sought their registration among those enrolled in the genealogies, but it was not found there, so they were excluded from the priesthood as unclean. The governor told them that they were not to partake of the most holy food until a priest with Urim and Thummim should arise. (7:64–65)

After listing priests and Levites, the record identifies three clans of laymen and three clans of priests who could not prove their lineage (7:61–63). Perhaps this was due to lapse of time since the exile. These priests were excluded from their duties until lots could be cast to determine the validity of their claim.

The question for us is this: Do we screen those we place in positions of leadership or service to ensure they are saved and are mature enough to be given responsibility? The principle here is the protection of the body of Christ.

Beloved, although I was very eager to write to you about our common salvation, I found it necessary to write appealing to you to contend for the faith that was once for all delivered to the saints. For certain people have crept in unnoticed who long ago were designated for this condemnation, ungodly people, who pervert the grace of our God into sensuality and deny our only Master and Lord, Jesus Christ. (Jude 3–4)

Personal Walls and Gates: When did you accept Jesus as Savior? Do you have assurance of your salvation? When did you make Jesus the Lord of your life? First Peter 2:9 tells us that we are "a royal priesthood." Is there evidence of that in our life?

Community Walls and Gates: Do we make it a practice to require clear testimonies before assigning teaching responsibilities? Do you consider Paul's list of qualifications for elders and deacons and their wives in 1 Timothy 3?

Disciples are discerning.

The Number Returning from Exile

The whole assembly together was 42,360, besides their male and female servants, of whom there were 7,337. And they had 245 singers, male and female. Their horses were 736, their mules 245, their camels 435, and their donkeys 6,720. (7:66–69)

These are the totals of those returning from the Babylonian exile, including their work animals.

We count members, attendance, salvations, baptisms, and giving as measures of church health. When the numbers go up, we are encouraged. Numbers are important throughout scripture as in the above verses.

Unfortunately, we fall into the trap of thinking that we are responsible for the increase. It is the Lord who brings the harvest. Do we make quantity more important than quality? Is making disciples a priority?

> And the Lord added to their number day by day those who were being saved. (Acts 2:47)

Personal Walls and Gates: How do you measure success in your life? Do you view success as the world does or from a spiritual perspective: obedience?

Community Walls and Gates: Is disciple-making a priority? Are people being saved (the work of the Holy Spirit)? Are people moving from wide to deep in their spiritual life?

Disciples celebrate new life.

Giving to the Work

> Now some of the heads of fathers' houses gave to the work. The governor gave to the treasury 1,000 darics of gold, 50 basins, 30 priests' garments and 500 minas of silver. And some of the heads of fathers' houses gave into the treasury of the work 20,000 darics of gold and 2,200 minas of silver. And what the rest of the people gave was 20,000 darics of gold, 2,000 minas of silver, and 67 priests' garments. (7:70–72)

The people contributed to the operation of the temple. The giving involved money and priestly garments.

Nehemiah states twice that "some of the heads of the families contributed to the work." He also states that the rest of the people also contributed. It is likely that the "heads of the fathers' houses" collected what was given from the clans. Some gave abundantly. They gave items they brought from Babylon. Cyrus opened his treasury to support the work of the temple and returned the "articles of the house of the Lord" to the returning exiles (Ezra 1:7–11).

We can be easily distracted by the things of the world. Do we let our perceived needs take precedence over giving to the Lord? We too frequently fail to recognize that everything that we possess, even the very breath of life, comes from the Lord.

> The point is this: whoever sows sparingly will also reap sparingly, and whoever sows bountifully will also reap bountifully. Each one must give as he has decided in his heart, not reluctantly or under compulsion, for God loves a cheerful giver. (2 Corinthians 9:6–7)

Personal Walls and Gates: How hard do you hold onto "stuff"? Do you understand at the action level that it all comes from the Lord?

Community Walls and Gates: Do you teach that giving is a part of discipleship?

Disciples give willingly.

Returning to the City for the Feasts of Tishri

> So the priests, the Levites, the gatekeepers, the singers, some of the people, the temple servants, and all Israel, lived in their towns. And when the seventh month had come, the people of Israel were in their towns. (7:73) And all the people gathered as one man into the square before the Water Gate. And they told Ezra the scribe to bring the Book of the Law of Moses that the LORD had commanded Israel. So Ezra the priest brought the Law before the assembly, both men and women and all who could understand what they heard, on the first day of the seventh month. (8:1–2)

The population of Jerusalem was decimated during Nebuchadnezzar's sieges. Therefore, Nehemiah enlisted workers from the surrounding region to build the walls and gates. Once that effort was completed, the workers returned to their homes. Then four days later, they returned to Jerusalem for the beginning of the fall feasts (the month of Tishri).

They hardly had time to recover from their labors. The calendar does not change, and God's instructions are permanently linked to the calendar. God's call on our lives is a call to a spiritual routine.

> Now Peter and John were going up to the temple at the hour of prayer, the ninth hour. (Acts 3:1)

Personal Walls and Gates: Does your calendar reflect your relationship with the Lord? What times and events take priority: quiet time, fellowship with believers, and service to others? Are you where you are supposed to be in your walk with the Lord? Are you serving where he wants you?

Community Walls and Gates: Are those in your sphere of influence where they need to be personally, relationally, and in service?

Disciples are disciplined.

SPIRITUAL RESTORATION

The Reading of the Law

> And all the people gathered as one man into the square before the Water Gate. And they told Ezra the scribe to bring the Book of the Law of Moses that the LORD had commanded Israel. So Ezra the priest brought the Law before the assembly, both men and women and all who could understand what they heard, on the first day of the seventh month. And he read from it facing the square before the Water Gate from early morning until midday, in the presence of the men and the women and those who could understand. And the ears of all the people were attentive to the Book of the Law. (8:1–3)

During the seventh month of the Jewish calendar, the Lord established three feasts and a solemn assembly. On the first of the month was the Feast of Trumpets [Rosh Hashanah]. This was followed on the tenth day by the Day of Atonement (Yom Kippur) and the seven-day Feast of Tabernacles or Booths beginning on the fifteenth. This was followed immediately by a sacred assembly (Leviticus 23:26–36).

Ezra 3:4 indicated they celebrated the Feast of Tabernacles prior to the reconstruction of the temple. Perhaps in the intervening time between the exile and the arrival of Ezra and Nehemiah, and after several generations, the people had forgotten the feasts, specifically, the Feast of Tabernacles.

Possibly it was a lack of spiritual leadership; there was no one to lead worship and the celebration of the festivals.

It is important for believers to constantly be reminded of the need for obedience through a routine time in the Word, prayer, and fellowship. The Lord continually calls us from who we are to who he wants us to be.

> And let us consider how to stir up one another to love and good works, not neglecting to meet together, as is the habit of some, but encouraging one another, and all the more as you see the Day drawing near. (Hebrews 10:24–25)

Personal Walls and Gates: Does your time in prayer and the Word direct you on the path God has set for you? Are you pursuing that call? Do you routinely gather with others to hear the Word and pray?

Community Walls and Gates: Are you gentle in reminding others not to neglect time in prayer, the Word, and coming together?

Disciples routinely come together in the Word.

Hearing the Word

> And Ezra the scribe stood on a wooden platform
> that they had made for the purpose. And beside
> him stood Mattithiah, Shema, Anaiah, Uriah,
> Hilkiah, and Maaseiah on his right hand, and
> Pedaiah, Mishael, Malchijah, Hashum,
> Hashbaddanah, Zechariah, and Meshullam on his
> left hand. And Ezra opened the book in the sight
> of all the people, for he was above all the people,
> and as he opened it all the people stood. And
> Ezra blessed the LORD, the great God, and all the
> people answered, "Amen, Amen," lifting up their
> hands. And they bowed their heads and
> worshiped the LORD with their faces to the
> ground. (8:4–6)

You would think that with the walls and gates completed they would have a dedication and celebrate. However, the prescribed feasts of the month of Tishri, the seventh month, took priority.

Moreover, the Lord required the reading of the Law every seven years.[31] It is uncertain if this reading of the Law was on the seven-year cycle or a reestablishment of the practice. However, the focus of the book of Nehemiah turns to Ezra, a priest and "skilled scribe in the law of Moses" (Ezra 7:6).

It was the custom of the people to stand for the reading of the Law. When Ezra pronounced the blessing or benediction prior to reading, the people responded by lifting their hands and then fell in worship.

> And they fell on their faces before the throne and worshiped God, saying, "Amen! Blessing and glory and wisdom and thanksgiving and honor and power and might be to our God forever and ever! Amen." (Revelation 7:11–12)

Personal Walls and Gates: What are the priorities in your spiritual life? Are certain times and events more important than others? Where does the work of the Lord and your relationship with him fit into the pattern of your life?

Community Walls and Gates: Are people around you running on empty? Do they need encouragement to stop and strengthen or renew their relationship with the Lord?

Disciples put a priority on their relationship with the Lord.

Understanding the Law

> Also Jeshua, Bani, Sherebiah, Jamin, Akkub, Shabbethai, Hodiah, Maaseiah, Kelita, Azariah, Jozabad, Hanan, Pelaiah, the Levites, helped the people to understand the Law, while the people remained in their places. They read from the book, from the Law of God, clearly, and they gave the sense, so that the people understood the reading. (8:7–8)

These verses are understood to mean that the Law was read paragraph by paragraph ("distinctly" in the NKJV) and the Levites provided a paraphrase of the reading in Aramaic, the common language of the day, that is, they provided understanding. Some believe that the Levites helped by translating as they passed through the crowd because the people may not have understood Hebrew. (See 13:24.)[32]

In our services today, the scripture is read in the language of the people with an explanation based on study of the original Hebrew or Greek. The sermon or message may be developed to answer three questions: what does the passage say, what does it mean, and how is it to be applied? God's Word is given to be applied.

> But be doers of the word, and not hearers only, deceiving yourselves. For if anyone is a hearer of the word and not a doer, he is like a man who looks intently at his natural face in a mirror. For he looks at himself and goes away and at once forgets what he was like. But the one who looks into the perfect law, the law of liberty, and perseveres, being no hearer who forgets but a doer who acts, he will be blessed in his doing. (James 1:22–25)

Personal Walls and Gates: In reading the Word, do you stop to consider what it is saying, what it means, and how it applies personally and in terms of your calling?

Community Walls and Gates: Are there those in your sphere of influence who need a greater understanding of the Word? Do you engage in helping them gain that understanding? Do you suggest ways in which the Word can be applied?

Disciples hear and obey the Word.

Celebrate the Renewal

> And Nehemiah, who was the governor, and Ezra the priest and scribe, and the Levites who taught the people said to all the people, "This day is holy to the LORD your God; do not mourn or weep." For all the people wept as they heard the words of the Law. (8:9)

The people wept at hearing the Law. Why? Was it from guilt or remorse, or were they overwhelmed by hearing the Word of God? Regardless, the leadership considered it inappropriate. This was to be a time of celebration and joy. It was a time for renewing their covenant relationship with the Lord.

When we are in a right relationship with the Lord there should be joy. Praise and thanksgiving should flow from the heart. Restoration and renewal are cause for celebration.

> And to be renewed in the spirit of your minds, and to put on the new self, created after the likeness of God in true righteousness and holiness. (Ephesians 4:23–24)

Personal Walls and Gates: Is renewal a routine part of your walk with the Lord? Does counting your blessings bring joy?

Community Walls and Gates: Are you aware of people burdened by trials and turmoil? Do they need to be reminded to count their blessings?

Disciples are renewed daily.

Sharing the Bounty

> Then he said to them, "Go your way. Eat the fat and drink sweet wine and send portions to anyone who has nothing ready, for this day is holy to our Lord. And do not be grieved, for the joy of the LORD is your strength." So the Levites calmed all the people, saying, "Be quiet, for this day is holy; do not be grieved." And all the people went their way to eat and drink and to send portions and to make great rejoicing, because they had understood the words that were declared to them. (8:10–12)

The Feast of Trumpets was celebrated on the first day of the Jewish seventh month. It was held at the completion of the harvest.

Ezra urged the people to celebrate. Not just celebrate but celebrate with the best. Fat was usually a part of sacrifices to the Lord—the very best. Now they were told to eat the fat, which enhances the flavor, and to drink wine mixed with honey. It was to celebrate the abundance of the Lord's blessings and his protection.

Moreover, Ezra instructed the people to share with the less fortunate so they could be included in the celebration.

The Lord has blessed and protected us. Today we celebrate the abundance of the harvest at Thanksgiving and share with the less fortunate.

> For here we have no lasting city, but we seek the city that is to come. Through him then let us continually offer up a sacrifice of praise to God, that is, the fruit of lips that acknowledge his name. Do not neglect to do good and to share what you have, for such sacrifices are pleasing to God. (Hebrews 13:13–16)

Personal Walls and Gates: How do you celebrate the Lord's abundant provisions and protection? Is sharing with the less fortunate a part of your celebration?

Community Walls and Gates: Who in your community can be encouraged through sharing?

Disciples celebrate the Lord's blessings and share with others.

Discovering the Feast of Booths

> On the second day the heads of fathers' houses of all the people, with the priests and the Levites, came together to Ezra the scribe in order to study the words of the Law. And they found it written in the Law that the LORD had commanded by Moses that the people of Israel should dwell in booths during the feast of the seventh month, and that they should proclaim it and publish it in all their towns and in Jerusalem, "Go out to the hills and

bring branches of olive, wild olive, myrtle, palm, and other leafy trees to make booths, as it is written." So the people went out and brought them and made booths for themselves, each on his roof, and in their courts and in the courts of the house of God, and in the square at the Water Gate and in the square at the Gate of Ephraim. And all the assembly of those who had returned from the captivity made booths and lived in the booths, for from the days of Jeshua the son of Nun to that day the people of Israel had not done so. And there was very great rejoicing. (8:13–17).

"And they found written …" Clearly, obedience comes from time in the Word. The Feast of Tabernacles (Booths) had not been celebrated "since the days of Joshua" (8:17). This feast was instituted as a reminder of their temporary living arrangements during their 40 years in the desert.

However, scripture records that this feast had been celebrated on several occasions before (1 Kings 8:65; 2 Chronicles 7:9; and the previously mentioned Ezra 3:4). Most commentators explain the difference in terms of the exuberance of the celebration.[33]

The important point is that the people listened to the words being read and acted.

For the word of God is living and active, sharper than any two-edged sword, piercing to the division of soul and of spirit, of joints and of marrow, and discerning the thoughts and intentions of the heart. And no creature is hidden from his sight, but all are naked and exposed to the eyes of him to whom we must give account. (Hebrews 4:12–13)

Personal Walls and Gates: Is time in the Word a part of your routine? What is he asking you to do? Do you take God's instructions seriously?

Community Walls and Gates: Are any around you needing to hear the Word? Do they need to be encouraged to act on the Word?

Disciples are refreshed daily by the Word of God.

The Sacred Assembly

So the people went out and brought them and made booths for themselves, each on his roof, and in their courts and in the courts of the house of God, and in the square at the Water Gate and in the square at the Gate of Ephraim. And all the assembly of those who had returned from the captivity made booths and lived in the booths, for from the days of Jeshua the son of Nun to that day the people of Israel had not done so. And there was very great rejoicing. And day by day, from the first day to the last day, he read from the Book of the Law of God. They kept the feast seven days, and on the eighth day there was a solemn assembly, according to the rule. (8:16–18)

A sacred or solemn assembly followed the Feast of Tabernacles. Solemn assemblies were typically times of fasting and sacrifice. Here, it came at the conclusion of a great celebration. As we shall see in chapter 9, it was a time of great praise and thanksgiving.

It is important to set aside special times in our personal worship and in our churches to celebrate what God has done and is doing.

> But the hour is coming, and is now here, when the true worshipers will worship the Father in spirit and truth, for the Father is seeking such people to worship him. God is spirit, and those who worship him must worship in spirit and truth. (John 4:23–24)

Personal Walls and Gates: Do you set aside times in your personal life to reflect on what God is doing? Do you schedule special days on your personal calendar for prayer and fasting?

Community Walls and Gates: Does your fellowship set aside special times to reflect on what God is doing in the lives of individuals and the body of believers?

Disciples celebrate what God has done privately and publicly.

Solemn Assembly: Fasting, Sackcloth, and Dust

> Now on the twenty-fourth day of this month the people of Israel were assembled with fasting and in sackcloth, and with earth on their heads. (9:1)

The walls and gates had been completed. Ezra had read the Law to them, which brought them to grief over their sins and the sins of their fathers. Recall in verse 8:9 that they were told not to weep. Ahead of them were the celebrations of the Feast of Trumpets, the Day of Atonement, and the Feast of the Tabernacles.

The day after the Feast of Tabernacles, the people gathered in a solemn assembly. It was a day of confession and seeking God's grace. In it, they expressed great remorse over the sins of the nation and their own failure to keep the Law.

- Fasting: Scripture indicates that the seventh month, the month of Tishri, was a month of fasting (Ezra 21, 10:6; Zechariah 7:5).[34] The purpose of fasting was to devote time to spiritual reflection without distractions.
- Sackcloth: Clothing worn to express remorse or grief. It was a dark, course garment or goat hair covering the loins.[35]
- Earth or dust: The mourner would sit on the ground and pour dust over his head.[36]

Great remorse happens when we recognize at the heart level the great harm we have done to our relationship with the Lord and with others and have destroyed our testimony. Confession and repentance are required.

> Draw near to God, and he will draw near to you. Cleanse your hands, you sinners, and purify your hearts, you double-minded. Be wretched and mourn and weep. Let your laughter be turned to mourning and your joy to gloom. Humble

yourselves before the Lord, and he will exalt you.
(James 4:8)

Personal Walls and Gates: Have you let something into your life that has broken your relationship with the Lord or with others? When you realize that, how do you respond? What are your sackcloth and ashes? Is fasting a part of your confession?
Community Walls and Gates: How does your community of believers respond when you become aware that you are not evangelizing or discipling? How do you respond corporately to that understanding?

Disciples seek to restore their relationship with the Lord through confession and repentance.

Solemn Assembly: Separation

> And the Israelites separated themselves from all foreigners and stood and confessed their sins and the iniquities of their fathers. (9:2)

The Hebrews were called to live separately from "foreigners" or non-Jews in the land. They failed to do that and even married the occupants of the land. This is mentioned again in chapters 10 and 13. God called Israel to be separate from the people around them, even to the point of eliminating them (the book of Joshua). They paid dearly for their failure to do so.

As believers, we are a holy people (i.e., set apart from the world). If we fail to separate ourselves from the world, we are in jeopardy of becoming like the world. Our faith becomes diluted and meaningless. Note: There is a practical reason for removing foreigners from the solemn assembly. By separating non-Jews, they were removing those who were not a part of the sins of Israel and therefore could not confess sins they had not committed.

> I appeal to you therefore, brothers, by the mercies of God, to present your bodies as a living sacrifice, holy and acceptable to God, which is your spiritual worship. Do not be conformed to this world, but be transformed by the renewal of your mind, that by testing you may discern what is the will of God, what is good and acceptable and perfect. (Romans 12:1–2)

Personal Walls and Gates: Do you think and act like the world? Where have you failed to separate yourself from the world?

Community Walls and Gates: Are any around you contaminated by the world? Are they sensing separation from the Lord? Are you encouraging them in their faith?

Disciples are not conformed to this world.

Solemn Assembly: The Word and Worship

> And they stood up in their place and read from the Book of the Law of the LORD their God for a quarter of the day; for another quarter of it they made confession and worshiped the LORD their God. On the stairs of the Levites stood Jeshua, Bani, Kadmiel, Shebaniah, Bunni, Sherebiah,

Bani, and Chenani; and they cried with a loud
voice to the LORD their God. Then the Levites,
Jeshua, Kadmiel, Bani, Hashabneiah, Sherebiah,
Hodiah, Shebaniah, and Pethahiah, said, "Stand
up and bless the LORD your God from everlasting
to everlasting. Blessed be your glorious name,
which is exalted above all blessing and praise.
"You are the LORD, you alone. You have made
heaven, the heaven of heavens, with all their host,
the earth and all that is on it, the seas and all that
is in them; and you preserve all of them; and the
host of heaven worships you. (9:3–6)

The prayer in chapter 9 is acclaimed as one of the great Old
Testament prayers outside the psalms. This prayer
acknowledges Yahweh as creator and reviews the cycles of
disobedience in the history of Israel. The prayer also presents a
clear understanding of God's greatness, patience, and
faithfulness.

The Levites assisted Ezra in reading the Law and in
confessing the sins of the nation. They stood on platforms
throughout the area where the Israelites had gathered at the
Water Gate. Each read from the Law and began worshipping
the Lord in unison.[37]

The next eight verses celebrate how the Lord had blessed
the people, cared for them, and faithfully met their needs. The
prayer began with praise and thanksgiving, acknowledging who
God is.

Jesus instructed his followers to begin their prayers by
acknowledging the Father and glorifying him. Focusing on

God's greatness helps us understand the great void between God and us. We are not God—not even close.

> And what is the immeasurable greatness of his power toward us who believe, according to the working of his great might … (Ephesians 1:19)

Personal Walls and Gates: How long can you pray in your quiet time before starting to ask the Lord for something?
Community Walls and Gates: How quickly do you move from praise to petition in your corporate prayer?

Disciples glorify God.

The Solemn Assembly: Confession and Restoration

> But they and our fathers acted presumptuously and stiffened their neck and did not obey your commandments. They refused to obey and were not mindful of the wonders that you performed among them, but they stiffened their neck and appointed a leader to return to their slavery in Egypt. But you are a God ready to forgive, gracious and merciful, slow to anger and abounding in steadfast love, and did not forsake them. (9:16–17)

> Nevertheless, in your great mercies you did not make an end of them or forsake them, for you are a gracious and merciful God. (9:31)

Verses 16–31 alternate between a detailed chronological listing of Israel's failures to keep the covenant with the Lord and his faithfulness and mercy in forgiving and restoring them.

Clearly, the leadership understood the history of Israel and the failures of the people throughout the centuries. More importantly, they had a clear sense of God's love, patience, and faithfulness by looking back as if in a rearview mirror.

When looking at God in your rearview mirror, what do you see?

Smooth Places	**Potholes**
• salvation	• wanderings
• transformation	• broken commitments
• Friends and mentors	• failures
• deliverance	• seeking after things of the world
• protection	• bondage
• blessings	• thought life

God's patience, faithfulness, mercy, and forgiveness are unending despite Israel's and our failures.

- The faithful God: God is always there. He is the one who keeps his covenant. The Lord is the shepherd who is always seeking lost sheep and meeting the needs of the flock.
- The compassionate God: He hears the prayers of his people and responds. God pours out his compassion and mercy on those who seek him.
- The forgiving God: God continues to forgive despite

Israel's continuing disobedience. He does not hold the sins of past generations against the present generation. Each generation must seek its own peace with God.

> For I am sure that neither death nor life, nor angels nor rulers, nor things present nor things to come, nor powers, nor height nor depth, nor anything else in all creation, will be able to separate us from the love of God in Christ Jesus our Lord. (Romans 8:38–39)

Personal Walls and Gates: Where have you failed? Have you allowed the Lord to make teachable moments out of your failures? Do you rejoice with the Lord over the smooth places in the road? Does your rearview mirror indicate something you need to do?

Community Walls and Gates: Are there people in your life who need to see God at work in the rough spots? Are you sharing your testimony about your rough spots and how God carried you through?

For the disciple, the victory has been won!

The Solemn Assembly: Confession

> Now, therefore, our God, the great, the mighty, and the awesome God, who keeps covenant and steadfast love, let not all the hardship seem little to you that has come upon us, upon our kings,

our princes, our priests, our prophets, our fathers, and all your people, since the time of the kings of Assyria until this day. Yet you have been righteous in all that has come upon us, for you have dealt faithfully and we have acted wickedly. Our kings, our princes, our priests, and our fathers have not kept your law or paid attention to your commandments and your warnings that you gave them. Even in their own kingdom, and amid your great goodness that you gave them, and in the large and rich land that you set before them, they did not serve you or turn from their wicked works. Behold, we are slaves this day; in the land that you gave to our fathers to enjoy its fruit and its good gifts, behold, we are slaves. And its rich yield goes to the kings whom you have set over us because of our sins. They rule over our bodies and over our livestock as they please, and we are in great distress. (9:32–37)

The last verses of this prayer acknowledge God's patience and faithfulness to his people and the renewing of the covenant.

Man is always seeking something better through human means. The children of Israel failed to rid the land of pagans and therefore were always distracted by their neighbors, coveting what they had, seeking wives from their midst, and seeking a king. They followed all that glitters.

We are no different. We are distracted by the world and fall into Satan's traps. The good news is that God is always ready to rescue us regardless of where we are or what we have done. He is the Great Recycler. He restores us. He repeatedly makes us into useful instruments again. Do we accept that God can restore us? We live under a new covenant. We live under the blood shed by Christ on the cross.

> Therefore, my beloved brothers, be steadfast, immovable, always abounding in the work of the Lord, knowing that in the Lord your labor is not in vain. (1 Corinthians 15:58)

Personal Walls and Gates: Are there things in your life that distract you from pursuing God's calling? Do you stop to acknowledge that failure? Do you take time to renew your commitment to the Lord?

Community Walls and Gates: Does your community of believers acknowledge failure to reach the lost and to disciple others? Do you practice a corporate renewal of the covenant with the Lord?

Disciples reconnect and recommit to the Lord.

Renewal of the Covenant

> Because of all this we make a firm covenant in writing; on the sealed document are the names of our princes, our Levites, and our priests. On the seals are the names of Nehemiah the governor, the son of Hacaliah, Zedekiah, Seraiah, Azariah, Jeremiah, Pashhur, Amariah, Malchijah, Hattush, Shebaniah, Malluch ...

The rest of the people, the priests, the Levites, the gatekeepers, the singers, the temple servants, and all who have separated themselves from the peoples of the lands to the Law of God, their wives, their sons, their daughters, all who have knowledge and understanding, join with their brothers, their nobles, and enter into a curse and an oath to walk in God's Law that was given by Moses the servant of God, and to observe and do all the commandments of the LORD our Lord and his rules and his statutes. (9:38–10:29)

The people of Israel had seen God's hand in their return from exile, the rebuilding of the temple, and the completion of the walls and gates. They had heard the Law of God and confessed their sins. The solemn assembly continued with the eighty-four leaders signing a renewal of the covenant. The rest of the people followed by signifying their commitment to the covenant by oath or other form of consent.

By mentioning the Law given by Moses, they were acknowledging their failure to keep the covenant and "making a covenant to keep the covenant."[38] So serious was their commitment they placed themselves under a threat of severe penalty should they fail and then covered it by an oath.[39] The writer of Hebrews reminds us that we live under a new covenant.

"This is the covenant that I will make with them after those days, declares the Lord: I will put my laws on their hearts, and write them on their minds," then he adds, "I will remember their sins and their lawless deeds no more." Where there is forgiveness of these, there is no longer any offering for sin. (Hebrews 10:16)

Personal Walls and Gates: How often do you renew your commitment to the Lord? Do you put it in writing?
Community Walls and Gates: Does your fellowship renew its covenant to the Lord?

Disciples make a practice of renewing their commitment to the Lord.

Renewal of the Covenant: Separation

> We will not give our daughters to the peoples of the land or take their daughters for our sons. (10:30)

The first part of this covenant renewal was to keep the family pure. This included avoiding introducing anything into the family that was outside the will of God. They understood that they must not be unequally yoked in their social relationships as Paul advises in 2 Corinthians 6:14.

Today, we see the moral collapse of societies around the world due to the breakdown of the family.

> Do not be unequally yoked with unbelievers. For what partnership has righteousness with lawlessness? Or what fellowship has light with darkness? What accord has Christ with Belial? Or

what portion does a believer share with an unbeliever? What agreement has the temple of God with idols? For we are the temple of the living God. (2 Corinthians 6:14–16)

Personal Walls and Gates: Are you committed to your marriage covenant? Are there things in your life that do not glorify God? Do you make a conscious effort to keep your marriage and family pure?

Community Walls and Gates: Are you aware of those around you who are struggling with keeping their commitments pure? Are you covering that situation with prayer?

Disciples keep the family environment pure.

Renewal of the Covenant: Keeping the Sabbath Holy

And if the peoples of the land bring in goods or any grain on the Sabbath day to sell, we will not buy from them on the Sabbath or on a holy day. And we will forego the crops of the seventh year and the exaction of every debt. (10:31)

The second element of the renewal was a commitment not to buy anything on the Sabbath and other holy days. They also committed to a sabbatical year that entailed allowing the ground to lie fallow every seventh year.

The intent here was to avoid distractions on days the Lord called holy. Our focus should be on God's mercy, grace, power, and love and on who he is and who we are not. The Sabbath was a time for disciplined focus. Furthermore, the seven-year sabbatical was an extended period for renewal of the soil and the soul.

And he said to them, "The Sabbath was made for man, not man for the Sabbath. So the Son of Man is lord even of the Sabbath." (Mark 2:27–28)

Personal Walls and Gates: Are your Sundays a time of spiritual reflection? Do you carve out an extended period for reflection and the renewal of your soul?
Community Walls and Gates: Is renewal of the covenant a part of your community's calendar? Is it a time for setting things right?

Disciples set aside time for reflection and renewal.

Renewal of the Covenant: Giving to the Lord

We also take on ourselves the obligation to give yearly a third part of a shekel for the service of the house of our God: for the showbread, the regular grain offering, the regular burnt offering, the Sabbaths, the new moons, the appointed feasts, the holy things, and the sin offerings to make atonement for Israel, and for all the work of the house of our God. We, the priests, the Levites, and the people, have likewise cast lots for the wood offering, to bring it into the house of our God, according to our fathers' houses, at times appointed, year by year, to burn on the altar of the LORD our God, as it is written in the Law. (10:32–34)

The third component of the binding agreement dealt with supporting the operation of the temple: a third of a shekel annually to purchase items to be consumed during offerings and sacrifices including wood for the perpetual fire in the sanctuary.

The Lord instructed Moses to collect half a shekel from each adult for the temple (Exodus 30:11–16). There is speculation that this assessment was reduced to a third of a shekel due to economic conditions brought about by the exile, famine, and strife.[40]

Under the new covenant we are to meet the needs of the body of Christ with tithes and offerings.

> Let the elders who rule well be considered worthy of double honor, especially those who labor in preaching and teaching. For the Scripture says, "You shall not muzzle an ox when it treads out the grain," and, "The laborer deserves his wages." (1 Timothy 5:17–18)

Personal Walls and Gates: Is giving to the Lord an obligation or a privilege? Does the Lord guide your giving?
Community Walls and Gates: How does your community of believers define the work of the Lord? Does your giving go beyond Jerusalem to Judea, Samaria, and the end of the earth?

Disciples give freely to the work of the Lord.

Renewal of the Covenant: Firstfruits

> We obligate ourselves to bring the firstfruits of our ground and the firstfruits of all fruit of every

tree, year by year, to the house of the LORD; also to bring to the house of our God, to the priests who minister in the house of our God, the firstborn of our sons and of our cattle, as it is written in the Law, and the firstborn of our herds and of our flocks; and to bring the first of our dough, and our contributions, the fruit of every tree, the wine and the oil, to the priests, to the chambers of the house of our God; and to bring to the Levites the tithes from our ground, for it is the Levites who collect the tithes in all our towns where we labor. And the priest, the son of Aaron, shall be with the Levites when the Levites receive the tithes. And the Levites shall bring up the tithe of the tithes to the house of our God, to the chambers of the storehouse. (10:35–38)

The fourth element of the commitment was to acknowledge the Law's requirement to bring the firstfruits of the harvest and livestock. After spring and summer, when food supplies were probably running low, the first of the crops went to the house of the Lord. It was a step of faith believing more would come. The agreement continued by making a distinction between the tithe of crops and the giving of firstfruits. Both offerings were given to support the Levites and other workers serving in the temple.

Also, they were to bring their firstborn sons to the priest for dedication to the Lord.[41]
All were to give including the Levites and the temple staff.

In our culture and times, what are firstfruits? Are they the first expense from the paycheck?

For they gave according to their means, as I can testify, and beyond their means, of their own accord ... For if the readiness is there, it is acceptable according to what a person has, not according to what he does not have. (2 Corinthians 8:3, 12)

Personal Walls and Gates: Is your giving disciplined? Do you take your tithes and offering from the top (firstfruits), or do you give from what is left?
Community Walls and Gates: Does your fellowship give to ministries outside the body?

Disciples give from the top.

Renewal of the Covenant: Offerings
For the people of Israel and the sons of Levi shall bring the contribution of grain, wine, and oil to the chambers, where the vessels of the sanctuary are, as well as the priests who minister, and the gatekeepers and the singers. We will not neglect the house of our God. (10:39)

The Lord, speaking through Malachi, directed that the full tithe be brought into the storehouse, "that there may be food in my house. And thereby put me to the test, says the LORD of hosts, if I will not open the windows of heaven for you and pour down for you a blessing until there is no more need" (Malachi 3:10).

The Old Testament makes the distinction between tithes and offerings. Tithes were defined as 10 percent of crops or income. Offerings were articles designated for sacrifices. Today some consider offerings to be over and above the tithe. Some consider offerings to be sacrificial giving. Others specify that tithes go to the local body while offerings are for ministries outside the local body.

> We want you to know, brothers, about the grace of God that has been given among the churches of Macedonia, for in a severe test of affliction, their abundance of joy and their extreme poverty have overflowed in a wealth of generosity on their part. For they gave according to their means, as I can testify, and beyond their means, of their own accord, begging us earnestly for the favor of taking part in the relief of the saints— and this, not as we expected, but they gave themselves first to the Lord and then by the will of God to us. (2 Corinthians 8:1–5)

Personal Walls and Gates: How do you define tithes and offering? Is your giving sacrificial? Do you give based on faith? **Community Walls and Gates:** Is your fellowship a storehouse? Do your people give to ministries outside your fellowship?

Disciples give tithes and offerings for the work of the Lord.

Renewal of the Covenant: Legalism

The people had just made a commitment to live under God's covenant. James Hamilton suggests that some might consider this covenant to be legalism.[42] Or perhaps one might think the original covenant was legalistic.

Legalism is the mistaken belief that holy living is the path to salvation or is needed to "remain saved." It is the belief that salvation and holy living can be achieved by human effort. In addition, legalism is the judgment that others need or can correct their own behavior. Legalism is the failure to recognize that transformation is offered freely through Christ's shed blood on the cross. Again, the underlying attitude is that people can change behavior by their own efforts. Legalism is the opposite of grace. Legalism is the failure to understand that the intention of the Mosaic Law was to point to the need for Christ—a Savior.[43]

As Hamilton states in his commentary, this renewal of the covenant was a willing commitment by the people, not rules imposed by God. It is a covenant in response to having been redeemed— released from exile—and living under the promise of the coming Messiah.[44]

> Now before faith came, we were held captive under the law, imprisoned until the coming faith would be revealed. So then, the law was our guardian until Christ came, in order that we might be justified by faith. But now that faith has come, we are no longer under a guardian, for in Christ Jesus you are all sons of God, through faith. For as many of you as were baptized into Christ have put on Christ. (Galatians 3:23–27)

Personal Walls and Gates: Are you laboring in vain to obtain salvation? Are you laboring under the impression that a holy life can be achieved through self-discipline? Do you judge others by the above faulty lines of thinking?

Community Walls and Gates: What barriers to faith and holy living does your fellowship impose?

Disciples are saved and empowered by the Spirit.

Fill the City

> The city was wide and large, but the people within it were few, and no houses had been rebuilt. (7:4) Now the leaders of the people lived in Jerusalem. And the rest of the people cast lots to bring one out of ten to live in Jerusalem the holy city, while nine out of ten remained in the other towns. And the people blessed all the men who willingly offered to live in Jerusalem. (11:1–3)

The temple had been rebuilt and the walls restored. The above verses indicate that only a few people lived in Jerusalem. Historians indicate that the city suffered sieges, attacks, capture, and recapture multiple times.[45] Therefore, it was imperative to populate the city for defensive purposes. Moreover, in its present condition, it did not represent the city of the God of Israel.

We are engaged in spiritual warfare! We are under attack! It is important for our spiritual well-being that we join and celebrate being overcomers in Christ. We need to engage with those who have yet to experience saving grace.

Finally, be strong in the Lord and in the strength of his might. Put on the whole armor of God, that you may be able to stand against the schemes of the devil. For we do not wrestle against flesh and blood, but against the rulers, against the authorities, against the cosmic powers over this present darkness, against the spiritual forces of evil in the heavenly places. (Ephesians 6:10–12)

Personal Walls and Gates: Are you engaged in reaching the lost? Do you have a plan for doing that? Where, when, and how? **Community Walls and Gates:** Are you bringing outsiders into your fellowship? Do you have a plan for reaching "outsiders"?

Disciples stand firm together.

The Record of Resettlement

These are the chiefs of the province who lived in Jerusalem; but in the towns of Judah everyone lived on his property in their towns … (11:3–36)

Chapter 11 is a detailed record of those who volunteered, those who were selected to resettle in Jerusalem, and those who remained in their villages. First is the list of the sons of Judah and Benjamin who resettled in Jerusalem (11:3–24). Next was a list of the villages and towns where the sons of Judah and Benjamin lived (11:25–35). And then the list of Levites from Judah who were reassigned to live with the tribe of Benjamin (11:36).

People may not have wanted to live in Jerusalem because it had a history of being attacked. Secondly, there was the matter of economics; as a farming society, there was no land in the city to grow crops.[46] Moreover, the city was not habitable; there were no houses. (7:4)

Consider that those on this list either volunteered or were selected to move into the city. They moved out of their comfort zones and had to build houses and begin new lives.

In life, there are physical, emotional, and spiritual comfort zones. They are often anchors that keep us from what the Lord wants us to do, where he wants us to go, and when he wants us to move. Unfortunately, we fail to understand that he is the one who does the work. He is the hand in our glove.

> And so, from the day we heard, we have not ceased to pray for you, asking that you may be filled with the knowledge of his will in all spiritual wisdom and understanding, so as to walk in a manner worthy of the Lord, fully pleasing to him: bearing fruit in every good work and increasing in the knowledge of God; being strengthened with all power, according to his glorious might, for all endurance and patience with joy; giving thanks to the Father, who has qualified you to share in the inheritance of the saints in light. (Colossians 1:9–12)

Personal Walls and Gates: What is the Lord asking you to do? Where is he asking you to go? When is he wanting you there? Are you ready to move out of your comfort zone?

Community Walls and Gates: Is there a new ministry the Lord is asking your congregation to launch? Are you hesitating? Why?

Disciples are directed by faith.

Priests and Levites

> These are the priests and the Levites who came up with Zerubbabel the son of Shealtiel, and Jeshua: Seraiah, Jeremiah, Ezra …
>
> These were the chiefs of the priests and of their brothers in the days of Jeshua …
>
> And the chiefs of the Levites: Hashabiah, Sherebiah, and Jeshua the son of Kadmiel, with their brothers who stood opposite them, to praise and to give thanks …
>
> These were in the days of Joiakim the son of Jeshua son of Jozadak, and in the days of Nehemiah the governor and of Ezra, the priest and scribe. (12:1–26)

Chapter 12 lists priests and Levites who returned from captivity, the two generations that followed, and their roles in temple worship.[47]

There is continuity in this list. It is about staying the course over the years despite trials and tribulation. Continuity is about legacy. In this case, it is about fathers, sons, and grandsons in ministry. It was about taking roles and responsibilities seriously.

You then, my child, be strengthened by the grace that is in Christ Jesus, and what you have heard from me in the presence of many witnesses entrust to faithful men, who will be able to teach others also. (2 Tim 2:1–2)

Personal Walls and Gates: Are you building a legacy within your family or within the younger generation around you?

Community Walls and Gates: Is there a conscious effort to build a spiritual heritage within your fellowship of believers?

Disciples make disciples.

Dedication of the Wall: Priorities

The wall was completed at the end of the month of Elul (6:15) and the people returned to their homes (7:73). While the date of the dedication of the wall is not specified, we know that the people devoted themselves to hearing the reading of the Law and celebrating the Feast of Booths. Then on the twenty-fourth day of Tishri (9:1), the solemn assembly began and concluded with the sealing of the covenant. This was followed by the resettling of Jerusalem. Therefore, the dedication of the wall took place at least a month after its completion.

Clearly, Nehemiah and the leadership considered the activities and events of the month of Tishri to be more important than dedicating the wall.

We lead busy lives. We are hammered by the demands of work and the needs of families and friends. We are distracted by the things of the world. Unless we live by a well-established set of priorities, we fail to keep important things in front of us. Unless we put him first, our relationship with the Lord gets lost in the noise of our lives.

> And he said to him, "You shall love the Lord your God with all your heart and with all your soul and with all your mind. This is the great and first commandment. (Matthew 22:37–38)

Personal Walls and Gates: Are time in prayer, the Word, corporate worship, and fellowship with other believers a routine part of your life? Are you careful not to let distractions interfere?

Community Walls and Gates: In your fellowship, do you take time to hear what others are learning from the Word? Do you set aside time to share what the Lord is doing in the lives of your people?

Disciples put the things of the Lord first.

THE DEDICATION
OF THE WALL

Dedication of the Wall: The Gathering

And at the dedication of the wall of Jerusalem
they sought the Levites in all their places, to bring
them to Jerusalem to celebrate the dedication
with gladness, with thanksgivings and with
singing, with cymbals, harps, and lyres. And the
sons of the singers gathered together from the
district surrounding Jerusalem and from the
villages of the Netophathites; also from Beth- gilgal
and from the region of Geba and Azmaveth, for
the singers had built for themselves villages
around Jerusalem. (12:27–29)

Recall that after repopulating Jerusalem, the Levites were
sent to their assigned towns and villages. The Levites were
divided into twenty-four teams. Each team came to Jerusalem to
serve at the temple for two weeks out of the year. The remaining

fifty weeks they lived in their towns and villages.[48]

These verses tell us that all the Levites were called to participate in the dedication of the wall. In addition, singers and those who played musical instruments were directed to participate in the dedication. This was a joyful occasion. It was a holy celebration!

Holman suggests that this was not only a celebration of the completion of the wall but also the renewal of the people.[49] Rejoice in the Lord always; again I will say, rejoice. (Philippians 4:4)

Personal Walls and Gates: Do you experience God working in your life? Do you rejoice when the Lord leads you to the end of a task? Do you celebrate spiritual transformation? Do you rejoice in success?

Community Walls and Gates: Do you stop to celebrate when God brings an effort to completion? Is celebrating "God at work" a routine part of your worship?

Disciples rejoice in the Lord.

Dedication of the Wall: The Cleansing

> And the priests and the Levites purified themselves, and they purified the people and the gates and the wall. (12:30)

Purification is a rite that prepares a person or people for a holy activity. Here, it was an act of preparing the heart and soul for worship. It was the recognition of the sinful nature of the leaders, priests, and people who were preparing to worship the Lord.

Purification prior to the dedication indicates the common mind- set that everyone needed to be spiritually prepared for this great event. By this, they were putting the Lord himself at the center of the festivities.

On this side of the cross, the process of purification takes place through the recognition that our righteousness is like that of "filthy rags."[50] Therefore, purification comes through confession and repentance.

> And forgive us our sins, as we have forgiven those
> who sin against us. (Matthew 6:12 NLT)

Personal Walls and Gates: What is your process of purification? Is it a daily activity? Do you see your life as an act of worship? How do you prepare to worship?

Community Walls and Gates: What is the process of purification in your fellowship? How do you prepare the hearts of the people to worship the Lord?

Disciples routinely confess their sins.

Dedication of the Wall: The Celebration

> Then I brought the leaders of Judah up onto the wall and appointed two great choirs that gave thanks. One went to the south on the wall to the Dung Gate ... The other choir of those who gave thanks went to the north, and I followed them with half of the people, on the wall, above the Tower of the Ovens ... to ... the Gate of the

Guard. So both choirs of those who gave thanks stood in the house of God ... And the singers sang with Jezrahiah as their leader. And they offered great sacrifices that day and rejoiced, for God had made them rejoice with great joy; the women and children also rejoiced. And the joy of Jerusalem was heard far away. (12:31–43)

Nehemiah organized two processions. Both processions ended at the Valley Gate and then proceeded to the temple area. The Valley Gate was the starting point for Nehemiah's survey of the ruins. But because of the devastation at that time, he could not circle the city (2:13, 15).[51] Now the walls were complete, and the choirs were able to circle the city.

"Great sacrifices" were part of the celebration. Sacrifices were commanded by God. They were done twice a day by the priests in the temple for the sins of the people. They were celebrating the hand of God and his protection over them and success in restoring the walls and gates.

It is not difficult to imagine the great joy of the people. What is important, however, is that their joy was given to them by the Lord. Joy comes from the Lord. Happiness comes from circumstances.

As the Father has loved me, so have I loved you. Abide in my love. If you keep my commandments, you will abide in my love, just as I have kept my Father's commandments and abide in his love. These things I have spoken to you, that my joy may be in you, and that your joy may be full. (John 15:9–11)

Personal Walls and Gates: Do you stop to celebrate what God is doing in your life?

Community Walls and Gates: Does your fellowship stop to celebrate corporately what God is doing in the life of the church and the people? Does your celebration embrace the victory by "marching around the walls?"

Disciples celebrate the work of the Lord.

Service at the Temple

> On that day men were appointed over the storerooms, the contributions, the firstfruits, and the tithes, to gather into them the portions required by the Law for the priests and for the Levites according to the fields of the towns, for Judah rejoiced over the priests and the Levites who ministered. And they performed the service of their God and the service of purification, as did the singers and the gatekeepers, according to the command of David and his son Solomon. For long ago in the days of David and Asaph there were directors of the singers, and there were songs of praise and thanksgiving to God. And all Israel in the days of Zerubbabel and in the days of Nehemiah gave the daily portions for the singers and the gatekeepers; and they set apart that which was for the Levites; and the Levites set apart that which was for the sons of Aaron. (12:44–47)

"On that day"—when their hearts were filled with joy (12:43)— their thoughts turned to meeting the needs of the priests and Levites. After all, the priests and Levites led the celebration at the dedication of the wall. Moreover, supporting the work of the temple and the temple staff was required by the Law.

God gave them joy, and that joy spilled over into obedience and giving.

Hamilton points out that the generosity of the people came during a period of poor economic conditions.[52] It was not a time of prosperity. In fact, some were destitute. Therefore, giving was sacrificial for many.

> We want you to know, brothers, about the grace of God that has been given among the churches of Macedonia, for in a severe test of affliction, their abundance of joy and their extreme poverty have overflowed in a wealth of generosity on their part. For they gave according to their means, as I can testify, and beyond their means, of their own accord, begging us earnestly for the favor of taking part in the relief of the saints— and this, not as we expected, but they gave themselves first to the Lord and then by the will of God to us. (2 Corinthians 8:1–5)

Personal Walls and Gates: Have you experienced a joy that motivates you to greater devotion and service? Have you been inspired to give sacrificially?

Community Walls and Gates: Does your fellowship give to needs beyond itself? Is that giving out of a heartfelt obedience or a sense of obligation?

Disciples give from the heart.

NEHEMIAH' REFORMS

Reform One: Separating Those of Foreign Descent

> On that day they read from the Book of Moses in
> the hearing of the people. And in it was found
> written that no Ammonite or Moabite should
> ever enter the assembly of God, for they did not
> meet the people of Israel with bread and water but
> hired Balaam against them to curse them—yet
> our God turned the curse into a blessing. As soon
> as the people heard the law, they separated from
> Israel all those of foreign descent. (13:1–3)

Chapter 13 begins about twenty-two years after the
dedication of the wall.[53] Hamilton indicates that the wording
"on that day" in Hebrew suggests that a significant period had
passed since the conclusion of chapter 12.[54]

The reference to the Law was to Deuteronomy 23:3–6, which specified that no Ammonite or Moabite was permitted in the "assembly of the Lord" for the reasons stated in the verses above.

This is now the third time the Israelites had been called to separate themselves from foreigners.[55] But they went a step further by separating themselves from "all those of foreign descent."

As chapter 13 continues, we become aware of the destructive influence foreigners had on the Israelites.

Today we live in a culture that is antagonistic to the Lord and the life he calls us to live. Just as Israel did, we need to separate ourselves from ungodly influences. We need to have secure walls and gates to protect ourselves, our families, and our fellowship from "foreign" influence.

> I have given them your word, and the world has hated them because they are not of the world, just as I am not of the world. I do not ask that you take them out of the world, but that you keep them from the evil one. They are not of the world, just as I am not of the world. (John 17:14–15)

Personal Walls and Gates: How do you keep "foreign" influence from your life? How strong are your walls and gates?
Community Walls and Gates: How do you guard against the corruption of the world? What have you allowed into your fellowship that may corrupt the holiness of your fellowship?

Disciples build strong walls and gates.

Reform Two: Eliminating Corruption

> Now before this, Eliashib the priest, who was appointed over the chambers of the house of our God, and who was related to Tobiah, prepared for Tobiah a large chamber where they had previously put the grain offering, the frankincense, the vessels, and the tithes of grain, wine, and oil, which were given by commandment to the Levites, singers, and gatekeepers, and the contributions for the priests. While this was taking place, I was not in Jerusalem, for in the thirty-second year of Artaxerxes king of Babylon I went to the king. And after some time I asked leave of the king and came to Jerusalem, and I then discovered the evil that Eliashib had done for Tobiah, preparing for him a chamber in the courts of the house of God. And I was very angry, and I threw all the household furniture of Tobiah out of the chamber. Then I gave orders, and they cleansed the chambers, and I brought back there the vessels of the house of God, with the grain offering and the frankincense. (13:4–9)

Eliashib was the high priest (13:28). He gave Tobiah, an outspoken adversary of Israel and an Ammonite (4:3), a place to live in the temple. It appears likely that worship in the temple had ceased and the storehouse was empty.[56]

What happens to the people when the leadership is corrupt? Is there a connection between Eliashib's wickedness and the disobedience of the people described above?

Eliashib's actions profaned the house of the Lord. Moreover, his actions prevented storage of the provisions set aside for the Lord's servants.

Furthermore, his actions violated the commitment the people had made earlier (9:38, 10:37). Hamilton says, "This is a physical picture of spiritual reality."[57]

Nehemiah was not just angry; he was furious. Notice that he started his reforms by restoring or purifying the house of the Lord.

> Do you not know that you are God's temple and that God's Spirit dwells in you? If anyone destroys God's temple, God will destroy him. For God's temple is holy, and you are that temple. (1 Corinthians 3:16–17)

Personal Walls and Gates: What are you letting into the temple of God? How strong are your gates? Do you take time to evaluate God's temple and evict those things that corrupt your relationship with the owner of the temple?

Community Walls and Gates: Do you permit nonbelievers to defile God's house (those who might use them for inappropriate personal or secular activities)? Do you have a policy that defines who can use your facilities and for what purpose?

Disciples understand that they must keep the temple holy.

Reform Three: Providing for the Levites

> I also found out that the portions of the Levites
> had not been given to them, so that the Levites
> and the singers, who did the work, had fled each to
> his field. So I confronted the officials and said,
> "Why is the house of God forsaken?" And I
> gathered them together and set them in their
> stations. Then all Judah brought the tithe of the
> grain, wine, and oil into the storehouses. And I
> appointed as treasurers over the storehouses
> Shelemiah the priest, Zadok the scribe, and
> Pedaiah of the Levites, and as their assistant
> Hanan the son of Zaccur, son of Mattaniah, for
> they were considered reliable, and their duty was
> to distribute to their brothers. Remember me, O
> my God, concerning this, and do not wipe out my
> good deeds that I have done for the house of my
> God and for his service. (13:10–14)

Because the high priest gave the storeroom to Tobiah, there
was no place to store provisions for the Levites. The needs of the
Levites were not being met. Therefore, they worked the fields in
order to survive.

Nehemiah reinstated the storeroom and reinstituted the
tithe of grain, oil, and wine for the Levites. Because of the
corruption, he appointed reliable men to manage the storehouse.
Nehemiah restored the singers and Levites to their positions.

Today, our people give tithes and offerings with the
understanding that what is given will be well managed.

Those who are taught the word of God should provide for their teachers, sharing all good things with them. (Galatians 6:6 NLT)

Personal Walls and Gates: Is giving to support those who labor for the Lord a part of your personal or family budget?
Community Walls and Gates: Does your fellowship carefully screen those selected to oversee the counting of tithes and offerings? Are those who govern the use of tithes and offerings reliable?

Disciples provide for those who minister to them.

Reform Four: Keeping the Sabbath Holy (Part 1)

In those days I saw in Judah people treading winepresses on the Sabbath, and bringing in heaps of grain and loading them on donkeys, and also wine, grapes, figs, and all kinds of loads, which they brought into Jerusalem on the Sabbath day. And I warned them on the day when they sold food. Tyrians also, who lived in the city, brought in fish and all kinds of goods and sold them on the Sabbath to the people of Judah, in Jerusalem itself! Then I confronted the nobles of Judah and said to them, "What is this evil thing that you are doing, profaning the Sabbath day? Did not your fathers act in this way, and did not our God bring all this disaster on us and on this city? Now you are bringing more wrath on Israel by profaning the Sabbath." (13:15–18)

Nehemiah's reforms continued by removing those who sold goods on the Sabbath. When there was no worship at the temple, the people made the Sabbath just another day in the week.

The Lord intended the Sabbath to be a day for physical as well as spiritual rest. It was a time for worship and renewal.

Question: What happens if we fail to put first things first? Answer: They become second or third place and eventually have no place at all. Without spiritual discipline, without a spiritual routine, we rely on our own devices.

> For although they knew God, they did not honor him as God or give thanks to him, but they became futile in their thinking, and their foolish hearts were darkened. Claiming to be wise, they became fools, and exchanged the glory of the immortal God for images resembling mortal man and birds and animals and creeping things. (Romans 12:21–23)

Personal Walls and Gates: Do you have a daily "Sabbath"? How do you stay connected to truth? What is your spiritual routine?
Community Walls and Gates: As a body of believers, how do you encourage those on the fringe to make weekly worship a priority? Is there an intentional effort to build relationships with those on the fringe?

Disciples make time in prayer and the Word a priority.

Reform Five: Keeping the Sabbath Holy (Part 2)

> As soon as it began to grow dark at the gates of Jerusalem before the Sabbath, I commanded that the doors should be shut and gave orders that they should not be opened until after the Sabbath. And I stationed some of my servants at the gates, that no load might be brought in on the Sabbath day. Then the merchants and sellers of all kinds of wares lodged outside Jerusalem once or twice. But I warned them and said to them, "Why do you lodge outside the wall? If you do so again, I will lay hands on you." From that time on they did not come on the Sabbath. Then I commanded the Levites that they should purify themselves and come and guard the gates, to keep the Sabbath day holy. Remember this also in my favor, O my God, and spare me according to the greatness of your steadfast love. (13:19–22)

Nehemiah's second action in keeping the Sabbath holy was to shut the gates. This was a physical action with a spiritual impact. Nehemiah also removed the merchants waiting outside the city. Not only were the merchants not allowed to sell on the Sabbath, Nehemiah prohibited the merchants from being near the city on the Sabbath.

These verses are about temptation. Temptation is the mental image or thought that distracts from the spirit-filled life. The problem is not temptation itself; the problem is in acting on the temptation.

And lead us not into temptation but deliver us from evil (Matthew 6:13). Or, Keep us from pursing temptation.

Personal Gates: How do you handle temptation? How do you close the gate on temptation? Is the Holy Spirit active in closing the gates on that which is inappropriate?
Community Gates: Is your fellowship tempted to bring today's culture into the house of the Lord? Are you keeping the Sabbath holy?

Disciples have strong gates to counter temptation.

Reform Six: Keeping Marriage Holy

In those days also I saw the Jews who had married women of Ashdod, Ammon, and Moab. And half of their children spoke the language of Ashdod, and they could not speak the language of Judah, but only the language of each people. And I confronted them and cursed them and beat some of them and pulled out their hair. And I made them take an oath in the name of God, saying, "You shall not give your daughters to their sons, or take their daughters for your sons or for yourselves. Did not Solomon king of Israel sin on account of such women? Among the many nations there was no king like him, and he was beloved by his God, and God made him king over all Israel. Nevertheless, foreign women made even him to sin. Shall we then listen to you and do all this great evil and act treacherously against our God by marrying foreign women?" (13:23–26)

There are two problems here. First is the issue of the language. The Law was in Hebrew. If the people did not know Hebrew, how could they understand the law, the Lord's guidance, or direction? How could they know the Lord? Language is crucial to a culture. Under these circumstances, Hebrew could have become a dead language.

The second problem with the influence of foreign cultures is that God intended his people to be separate from the world. With intermarriage, the Hebrew culture would fade and eventually disappear.

God intended marriage to be the crucible for developing faith. Offspring from the marriage were to become immersed in the law as a hedge of protection against foreign influence. Moreover, parents were to model obedience to the Lord so that their children would learn obedience (faith).

> And these words that I command you today shall be on your heart. You shall teach them diligently to your children and shall talk of them when you sit in your house, and when you walk by the way, and when you lie down, and when you rise. You shall bind them as a sign on your hand, and they shall be as frontlets between your eyes. You shall write them on the doorposts of your house and on your gates. (Deuteronomy 6:6–9)

When the family is divided, there will be no consistent teaching.

> "Therefore, a man shall leave his father and mother and hold fast to his wife, and the two shall become one flesh." This mystery is profound, and I am saying that it refers to Christ and the church. However, let each one of you love his wife as himself, and let the wife see that she respects her husband. (Ephesians 5:31–33)

Personal Walls and Gates: What do you bring to your marriage? Are you careful to screen out the flawed influence of our secular culture? Is your family Christ-centered?

Community Walls and Gates: Does your fellowship emphasize Christ-centered family relationships? Do you have a marriage and family curriculum?

Disciples guard against foreign influence.

Reform Seven: Purifying the Priesthood

> And one of the sons of Jehoiada, the son of Eliashib the high priest, was the son-in-law of Sanballat the Horonite. Therefore I chased him from me. Remember them, O my God, because they have desecrated the priesthood and the covenant of the priesthood and the Levites. (13:28–29)

Nehemiah had just reestablished marriage as the means of keeping the people set apart and pure. Here, the son of the high priest was married to a foreigner. By tradition, he would become the next high priest. Not only that, he was the son-in-law of an enemy of the nation. His father was disobedient and the son was too.

It took only a matter of a few years for the Israelite society to become corrupted. It happens quickly when the leadership is corrupt.

> [An overseer] must manage his own household well, with all dignity keeping his children submissive, for if someone does not know how to manage his own household, how will he care for God's church? (1 Timothy 3:4–5)

Personal Walls and Gates: How do you keep the influence of an ungodly culture from gaining a foothold in your life? In your family? Are you training your children in the way they should go? (Proverbs 22:6)

Community Walls and Gates: How does the leadership of your congregation measure up to Paul's guidance to Timothy?

Disciples manage their families well.

Nehemiah's Prayer

> Thus I cleansed them from everything foreign, and I established the duties of the priests and Levites, each in his work; and I provided for the wood offering at appointed times, and for the firstfruits. Remember me, O my God, for good. (13:30–31)

When Nehemiah returned to Jerusalem from Susa, he found that the people had failed to keep the oath they had made to the Lord (chapter 10). He restored tithing. He selected trustworthy men to oversee the distribution of tithes and guard the gates on the Sabbath. He banished merchants from Jerusalem during the Sabbath. He made the men take an oath not to give their daughters, sons, and themselves in marriage to foreigners. He purified the priests and Levites and restored them to their duties and restored their support. We need to recognize the strength of Nehemiah's moral convictions and his insight into the consequences of sin. He was quick, bold, and determined in returning the people to the oath they had taken.

> But I am not ashamed, for I know whom I have believed, and I am convinced that he is able to guard until that day what has been entrusted to me. Follow the pattern of the sound words that you have heard from me, in the faith and love that are in Christ Jesus. By the Holy Spirit who dwells within us, guard the good deposit entrusted to you. (2 Timothy 1:12–14)

Personal Walls and Gates: Do you have the kind of devotional life that permits God to reveal the sin in your life? What action do you take when you fail to keep your promises to God? Do you take quick, bold, and aggressive action to seek God's forgiveness and then repent? Do you identify and remove "foreign" influences in your life?

Community Walls and Gates: Is the leadership of your fellowship firm in the faith? Are they ready to act when encountering "foreign" influence?

Disciples are empowered by the Holy Spirit.

Nehemiah's Reforms: A Summary

Notice the order of the reforms.
1. removing "foreigners"
2. cleansing the house of the Lord and restoring worship
3. providing for those who minister
4. keeping the Sabbath holy
5. removing interference with the Sabbath
6. keeping marriage holy
7. purifying the priesthood

Israel's problems always began by failing to be a separate people. What the walls were meant to keep out, the people let in through the gates. Reforms begin with eliminating "foreign" influence. It continues with restoring worship—both personal and corporate. It concludes with a time of confession and repentance.

But you are a chosen race, a royal priesthood, a holy nation, a people for his own possession, that you may proclaim the excellencies of him who called you out of darkness into his marvelous light. Once you were not a people, but now you are God's people; once you had not received mercy, but now you have received mercy.

> Beloved, I urge you as sojourners and exiles to abstain from the passions of the flesh, which wage war against your soul. Keep your conduct among the Gentiles honorable, so that when they speak against you as evildoers, they may see your good deeds and glorify God on the day of visitation. (1 Peter 2:9–11)

Personal Walls and Gates: What have you allowed into your life? What interferes with your obedience? What are the distractions in your life?

Community Walls and Gates: What practices of the world have infiltrated your worship and ministries? What practices have you adopted to attract people to your door?

Disciples maintain strong gates.

LEAVING A LEGACY

Nehemiah's Character

Nehemiah was a man of:

- Vision: He saw what was needed.
- Action: He led the rebuilding and reformation.
- Moral conviction: He acted on his convictions.
- Perseverance: He continued despite opposition.
- Prayer: He was quick to lay his problems before God.
- Discernment: He was quick to distinguish between right and wrong.
- Devotion to God: He continually sought to please and serve the Lord.
- Patience: He sought God's greater reward rather than man's quick but fleeting praise (Remember for my good, O my God, all that I have done for this people. (5:19)).
- Courage: He persisted in the face of opposition.
- Resolution: He never questioned what needed to be done.
  Nehemiah's family was removed from Judah by

Nebuchadnezzar in 586 BC. His family, four generations, lived in the pagan Babylonian culture for 140 years. In addition, Nehemiah served and, more than likely, lived in the court of Artaxerxes. Despite this, he and his family remained steadfast in their faith and obedience to the God of Israel. Nehemiah's unwavering faith allowed him to easily recognize the failures of the people and take quick action to put reforms in place.

Contrast this with the cycles of disobedience in Judah, just within the twenty-one-year period covered by the book of Nehemiah:

- They were easily corrupted by outside influence.
- They lacked discernment.
- They forgot the Law, and in doing so, they failed to put God first.
- The people lacked vision. They did not see the need to rebuild the walls and gates or considered it too difficult.
- They crumbled under threats from the opposition and were easily diverted from following their moral convictions.

Lesson One: Despite their continued failures and flagrant disobedience, God continued to restore them, knowing that they would fail again.

Lesson Two: Strong, faith-filled leadership in the home and community is key.

What was the legacy of the people? What was Nehemiah's legacy? As believers, what we leave behind is important, not in terms of riches but in terms of a steadfast faith that is poured into those who come behind: family, friends, new believers, and growing believers.

> But godliness with contentment is great gain, for
> we brought nothing into the world ... (1 Timothy
> 6:6–7)

Personal Walls and Gates: What will your legacy be? What will people remember about you?
Community Walls and Gates: Does your fellowship emphasize personal and corporate legacies?

Disciples leave a holy legacy.

NOTES

1 *History of Jerusalem*, Wikipedia,
https://en.m.wikipedia.org/wiki/History of Jerusalem, July 27, 2019.

2 Frank E. Gaebelein, ed., *The Expositor's Bible Commentary 5.0 for Windows* (Grand Rapids, Zondervan, n.d.), Nehemiah 1:3

3 *When and How Was Israel Conquered by the Assyrians?* https://www. gotquestions.org/Israel-conquered-by-Assyria.html.

4 "Artaxerxes I: King of Persia," *Encyclopedia Britannica*, https://www.britannica. com/biography/Artaxerxes-I, July 27, 2019.

5 Kidner, Derek, <u>*Ezra and Nehemiah: An Introduction and Commentary*</u>, vol. 12 (Downers Grove, IL: InterVarsity Press 1979) 83–84.

6 John MacArthur, Grace to You, www.gty.org/library/bible-introducations/ MSB16/nehemiah, 2. July 13, 2019.

7 Robert Jamieson; A. R. Faust; David Brown, *A Commentary, Critical, Experimental, and Practical on the Old and New Testament, Vol. II: Joshua– Esther* (London; Glasgow: William Collins, Sons, & Company, Limited, n.d.) 630–631.

8 Gaebelein, Nehemiah 13:6.

9 The Jewish Calendar vs. Gregorian Calendar, http://s4ctroops.com/id45. html.

10 Gaebelein, Nehemiah 2:10.

11 Breneman, M., *New American Commentary, Vol. 10, Ezra–Esther*, electronic ed. (Nashville: Broadman & Holman Publishers, 1993), 178.

12 Gaebelein, Nehemiah 2:13.

13 Breneman, 184.

14 Breneman, 195–196.

15 Gaebelein, Nehemiah 4:19.

16 Gaebelein, Nehemiah 5: Introduction, 1, 3.

17 James M. Hamilton Jr., *Ezra and Nehemiah* (Nashville, Holman, 2014), 126.

18 Getz, G. A. (1985). Nehemiah. In J. F. Walvoord and R. B. Zuck (Eds.), *The Bible Knowledge Commentary: An Exposition of the Scriptures*, vol. 1 (Wheaton, IL: Victor Books, 1985), 684.

19 Gaebelein, Nehemiah 5:12–13.

20 Matthew Henry, *Commentary on the Whole Bible, One Volume Edition* (Grand Rapids, Zondervan, 1960), 496.

21 Gaebelein, Nehemiah 6:9.

22 Breneman, 211–212.

23 Holman Study Bible, NKJV Edition (Nashville, Holman, 2013), 779.

24 Getz, 686.

25 Gaebelein, Nehemiah 6:15.

26 Breneman, 215–216, Holman, 780.

27 Kidner, 111.

28 Breneman, 216.

29 Gaebelein, Nehemiah 7:6–63.

30 *What Is the Importance of Genealogies in the Bible?* (www.compellingtruth. org/Bible-genealogies.html, August 2, 2019.

31 Jamieson, 618–619.

32 Hamilton, 156.

33 ESV Study Bible (Wheaton, Crossway, 2008), 837–8.

34 Gaebelein, Nehemiah 9:1.

35 R. Laird Harris, Gleason L. Archer Jr., Bruce K. Waltkey, *Theological Wordbook of the Old Testament, Vol. I* (Chicago, Moody, 1980), 883.

36 Gaebelein, Nehemiah 9:1.

37 Nehemiah 8:7–9 states that the listed Levites "helped the people understand the Law …" Therefore, it is likely that the Levites assisted in reading this great prayer. That would mean that they were reading from a previously prepared text.

38 Hamilton, 185.

39 Hamilton, 191.

40 Jamieson, 624.

41 Bible.org, *What Is the Significance of the First Born in the Bible?* https://bible.org/ question/what-significance-%E2%80%9Cfirstborn%E2%80%9D-bible, June 14, 2019.

42 Hamilton, 196.

43 Matt Slick, *What Is Legalism*, CARM, https://carm.org/what-is-legalism, June 13, 2019.

44 Hamilton, 191.

45 Mandy Katz, Moment, March–April 2008, *Do We Divide the Holiest Holy City?* https://web.archive.org/web/20080603214950/http://www.mo mentmag. com/Exclusive/2008/2008–03/200803–Jerusalem.html, June 21, 2019.

46 Hamilton, 202.

47 Kidner, 133.

48 Hamilton, 207.

49 Holman, 792.

50 Isaiah 64:6.

51 Hamilton, 208.

52 Hamilton, 211.

53 See "Introduction."

54 Hamilton, 216.

55 Ezra 9–10; Nehemiah 9:2.

56 Jamieson, 630.

57 Hamilton, 218.